More praise for Rollo May

❀

Love and Will

"Wise, rich, witty and indispensable. . . . It should have led any list of important books."　　　　　—John Leonard, *New York Times*

"An extraordinary book on sex and civilization. . . . An important contribution to contemporary morality."　　　　　—*Newsweek*

"A distillation of 25 years of front line service to individuals caught in the psychological cross-currents of this age of transition. . . . Dynamic, warm and compassionate!"　　　　　—*St. Louis Post-Dispatch*

"Dr. May offers an intensity and an intelligence that might make a difference in all our lives. *Love and Will* is a book to study and cherish, for those daring enough to study and cherish our human heritage and potential."　　　　　—*San Francisco Examiner*

"This volume—written in a brilliant and impeccable style—is an excellent analysis of life and love in the modern period, and is full of suggestive and encouraging insight."　　　　　—*Chicago Sun-Times*

"The implications of this distinguished book for education and culture are profound."　　　　　—*Harvard Educational Review*

The Courage to Create

"A lucid and highly concentrated analysis of the creative process. . . . [May] describes the requisites for the creative encounter and the moment of the 'breakthrough.'"　　　　　—*Saturday Review*

MAN'S SEARCH FOR HIMSELF

Rollo May, Ph.D.

W · W · NORTON & COMPANY
NEW YORK · LONDON

For information about permission to reproduce selections from this book, write to
Permissions, W. W. Norton & Company, Inc.,
500 Fifth Avenue, New York, NY 10110

For information about special discounts for bulk purchases, please contact
W. W. Norton Special sales at specialsales@wwnorton.com or 800-233-4830

Manufacturing by LSC Harrisonburg
Production manager: Devon Zahn

Library of Congress Cataloging-in-Publication Data

May, Rollo.
Man's search for himself / Rollo May.
p. cm.
Originally published: 1st ed. New York : Norton, c1953.
Includes bibliographical references and index.
ISBN 978-0-393-33315-2 (pbk.)
1. Self-perception. I. Title.
BF697.5.S43M29 2009
150.19'2—dc22

2008007363

W. W. Norton & Company, Inc., 500 Fifth Avenue, New York, N.Y. 10110
www.wwnorton.com

W. W. Norton & Company Ltd.
15 Carlisle Street, London W1D 3BS

1 2 3 4 5 6 7 8 9 0

Contents

✻

Preface

❋

ONE of the few blessings of living in an age of anxiety is that we are forced to become aware of ourselves. When our society, in its time of upheaval in standards and values, can give us no clear picture of "what we are and what we ought to be," as Matthew Arnold puts it, we are thrown back on the search for ourselves. The painful insecurity on all sides gives us new incentive to ask, Is there perhaps some important source of guidance and strength we have overlooked?

I realize, of course, that this is not generally called a blessing. People ask, rather, How can anyone attain inner integration in such a disintegrated world? Or they question, How can anyone undertake the long development toward self-realization in a time when practically nothing is certain, either in the present or the future?

Most thoughtful people have pondered these questions. The psychotherapist has no magic answers. To be sure, the new light which depth-psychology throws on the buried motives which make us think and feel and act the way we do should be of crucial help in one's search for one's self. But there is something in addition to his technical training and his own self-understanding which gives an author the courage to rush in where angels fear to tread and offer his ideas and experience on the difficult questions which we shall confront in this book.

This something is the wisdom the psychotherapist gains in working with people who are striving to overcome their problems. He has the extraordinary, if often taxing, privilege of accompanying persons through their intimate and profound struggles to gain new integration. And dull indeed would be the therapist who did not get glimpses into what blinds people in our day from themselves, and what blocks them in finding values and goals they can affirm.

Alfred Adler once said, referring to the children's school he had founded in Vienna, "The pupils teach the teachers." It is always thus in psychotherapy. And I do not see how the therapist can be anything but deeply grateful for what he is daily taught about the issues and dignity of life by those who are called his patients.

I am also grateful to my colleagues for the many things I have learned from them on these points; and to the students and faculty of Mills College in California for their rich and stimulating reactions when I discussed some of these ideas with them in my Centennial lectures there on "Personal Integrity in an Age of Anxiety."

This book is not a substitute for psychotherapy. Nor is it a self-help book in the sense that it promises cheap and easy cures overnight. But in another worthy and profound sense every good book is a self-help book—it helps the reader, through seeing himself and his own experiences reflected in the book, to gain new light on his own problems of personal integration. I hope this is that kind of book.

In these chapters we shall look not only to the new insights of psychology on the hidden levels of the self, but also to the wisdom of those who through the ages, in the fields of literature, philosophy, and ethics, have sought to understand how man can best meet his insecurity and personal crises, and turn them to constructive uses. Our aim is to discover ways in which we can stand against the insecurity of our time, to find a center of strength within ourselves, and as far as we can, to point the way toward achieving values and goals which can be depended upon in a day when very little is secure.

ROLLO MAY
NEW YORK CITY

MAN'S SEARCH FOR HIMSELF

To venture causes anxiety, but not to venture is to lose one's self.
. . . And to venture in the highest sense is precisely to become conscious of one's self.

—*Kierkegaard*

The one goeth to his neighbor because he seeketh himself, and the other because he would fain lose himself. Your bad love to yourselves maketh solitude a prison to you.

—*Nietzsche*

Part 1

OUR PREDICAMENT

1

The Loneliness and Anxiety
of Modern Man

WHAT are the major, inner problems of people in our day? When we look beneath the outward occasions for people's disturbances, such as the threat of war, the draft, and economic uncertainty, what do we find are the underlying conflicts? To be sure, the symptoms of disturbance which people describe, in our age as in any other, are unhappiness, inability to decide about marriage or vocations, general despair and meaning-lessness in their lives, and so on. But what underlies these symptoms?

At the beginning of the twentieth century, the most common cause of such problems was what Sigmund Freud so well described—the person's difficulty in accepting the instinctual, sexual side of life and the resulting conflict between sexual impulses and social taboos. Then in the 1920's Otto Rank wrote that the underlying roots of people's psychological problems at that time were feelings of inferiority, inade-quacy and guilt. In the 1930's the focus of psychological conflict shifted again: the common denominator then, as Karen Horney pointed out, was hostility between individuals and groups, often connected with the competitive feelings of who gets ahead of whom. What are the root problems in our middle of the twentieth century?

The Hollow People

It may sound surprising when I say, on the basis of my own clinical practice as well as that of my psychological and psychiatric colleagues, that the chief problem of people in the middle decade of the twentieth century is *emptiness*. By that I mean not only that many people do not know what they want; they often do not have any clear idea of what they feel. When they talk about lack of autonomy, or lament their inability to make decisions—difficulties which are present in all decades—it soon becomes evident that their underlying problem is that they have no definite experience of their own desires or wants. Thus they feel swayed this way and that, with painful feelings of power-lessness, because they feel vacuous, empty. The complaint which leads them to come for help may be, for example, that their love relationships always break up or that they cannot go through with marriage plans or are dissatisfied with the marriage partner. But they do not talk long before they make it clear that they expect the marriage partner, real or hoped-for, to fill some lack, some vacancy within themselves; and they are anxious and angry because he or she doesn't.

They generally can talk fluently about what they *should* want—to complete their college degrees successfully, to get a job, to fall in love and marry and raise a family—but it is soon evident, even to them, that they are describing what others, parents, professors, employers, expect of them rather than what they themselves want. Two decades ago such external goals could be taken seriously; but now the person realizes, even as he talks, that actually his parents and society do not make all these requirements of him. In theory at least, his parents have told him time and again that they give him freedom to make decisions for himself. And furthermore the person realizes himself that it will not help him to pursue such external goals. But that only makes his problem the more difficult, since he has so little conviction or sense of the reality of his own goals. As one person put it, "I'm just a collection of mirrors, reflecting what everyone else expects of me."

In previous decades, if a person who came for psychological help did not know what he wanted or felt, it generally could be assumed that he wanted something quite definite, such as some sexual grati-fication, but he dared not admit this to himself. As Freud made clear, the desire was there; the chief thing necessary was to clear up the repressions, bring the desire into consciousness, and eventually help the patient to become able to gratify his desire in accord with reality. But in our day sexual taboos are much weaker; the Kinsey report made that clear if anyone still doubted it. Opportunities for sexual gratification can be found without too much trouble by persons who do not have pronounced other problems. The sexual problems people bring today for therapy, furthermore, are rarely struggles against social prohibitions as such, but much more often are deficiencies within themselves, such as the lack of potency or the lack of capacity to have strong feelings in responding to the sexual partner. In other words, the most common problem now is not social taboos on sexual activity or guilt feeling about sex in itself, but the fact that sex for so many people is an empty, mechanical and vacuous experience.

A dream of a young woman illustrates the dilemma of the "mirror" person. She was quite emancipated sexually, but she wanted to get married and could not choose between two possible men. One man was the steady, middle-class type, of whom her well-to-do family would have approved; but the other shared more of her artistic and Bohemian interests. In the course of her painful bouts of indecision, during which she could not make up her mind as to what kind of person she really was and what kind of life she wished to lead, she dreamt that a large group of people took a vote on which of the two men she should marry. During the dream she felt relieved—this was certainly a convenient solution! The only trouble was when she awoke she couldn't remember which way the vote had gone.

Many people could say out of their own inner experience the prophetic words T. S. Eliot wrote in 1925:

We are the hollow men
We are the stuffed men
Leaning together
Headpiece filled with straw. Alas!

Shape without form, shade without colour,
Paralyzed force, gesture without motion; . . .*

* "The Hollow Men," in *Collected Poems*, New York, Harcourt, Brace and Co., 1934, p. 101.

Perhaps some readers are conjecturing that this emptiness, this inability to know what one feels or wants, is due to the fact that we live in a time of uncertainty—a time of war, military draft, economic change, with a future of insecurity facing us no matter how we look at it. So no wonder one doesn't know what to plan and feels futile! But this conclusion is too superficial. As we shall show later, the problems go much deeper than these occasions which cue them off. Furthermore, war, economic upheaval and social change are really symptoms of the same underlying condition in our society, of which the psychological problems we are discussing are also symptoms.

Other readers may be raising another question: "It may be true that people who come for psychological help feel empty and hollow, but aren't those *neurotic* problems, and not necessarily true for the majority of people?" To be sure, we would answer, the persons who get to the consulting rooms of psychotherapists and psychoanalysts are not a cross-section of the population. By and large they are the ones for whom the conventional pretenses and defenses of the society no longer work. Very often they are the more sensitive and gifted members of the society; they need to get help, broadly speaking, because they are less successful at rationalizing than the "well-adjusted" citizen who is able for the time being to cover up his underlying conflicts. Certainly the patients who came to Freud in the 1890's and the first decade of this century with the sexual symptoms he described were not representative of their Victorian culture: most people around them went on living under the customary taboos and rationalizations of Victorianism, believing that sex was repugnant and should be covered up as much as possible. But after the First World War, in the 1920's, those sexual problems became overt and epidemic. Almost every sophisticated person in Europe and America then experienced the same conflicts between sexual urges and social taboos which the few had been struggling with a decade or two earlier. No matter how highly one thinks of Freud, one would not be naive enough to suggest that he in his writings caused this development; he merely predicted it. Thus a relatively small number of people— those who come for psychotherapeutic help in the process of their

struggle for inner integration—provide a very revealing and significant barometer of the conflicts and tensions under the psychological
surface of the society. This barometer should be taken seriously, for it
is one of the best indexes of the disruptions and problems which have
not yet, but may soon, break out widely in the society.

Furthermore, it is not only in the consulting rooms of psychologists and psychoanalysts that we observe the problem of modern
man's inner emptiness. There is much sociological data to indicate that
the "hollowness" is already cropping out in many different ways in
our society. David Riesman, in his excellent book, *The Lonely Crowd*,
which came to my attention just as I was writing these chapters,
finds the same emptiness in his fascinating analysis of the present
American character. Before World War I, says Riesman, the typical
American individual was "inner-directed." He had taken over the
standards he was taught, was moralistic in the late Victorian sense,
and had strong motives and ambitions, derived from the outside
though they were. He lived as though he were given stability by an
inner gyroscope. This was the type which fits the early psychoanalytic
description of the emotionally repressed person who is directed by
a strong superego.

But the present typical American character, Riesman goes on to
say, is "outer-directed." He seeks not to be outstanding but to "fit in";
he lives as though he were directed by a radar set fastened to his head
perpetually telling him what other people expect of him. This radar
type gets his motives and directions from others; like the man who
described himself as a set of mirrors, he is able to respond but not to
choose; he has no effective center of motivation of his own.

We do not mean—nor does Riesman—to imply an admiration
for the inner-directed individuals of the late Victorian period. Such
persons gained their strength by internalizing external rules, by
compartmentalizing will power and intellect and by repressing their
feelings. This type was well suited for business success, for, like the
nineteenth-century railroad tycoons and the captains of industry,
they could manipulate people in the same way as coal cars or the stock
market. The gyroscope is an excellent symbol for them since it stands

for a completely mechanical center of stability. William Randolph Hearst was an example of this type: he amassed great power and wealth, but he was so anxious underneath this appearance of strength, particularly with regard to dying, that he would never allow anyone to use the word "death" in his presence. The gyroscope men often had disastrous influences on their children because of their rigidity, dogmatism, and inability to learn and to change. In my judgment the attitudes and behavior of these men are examples of how certain attitudes in a society tend to crystallize rigidly just before they collapse. It is easy to see how a period of emptiness would have to follow the breakdown of the period of the "iron men"; take out the gyroscope, and they are hollow.

So we shed no tears for the demise of the gyroscope man. One might place on his tombstone the epitaph, "Like the dinosaur, he had power without the ability to change, strength without the capacity to learn." The chief value in our understanding these last representatives of the nineteenth century is that we shall then be less likely to be seduced by their pseudo "inner strength." If we clearly see that their gyroscope method of gaining psychological power was unsound and eventually self-defeating, and their inner direction a moralistic substitute for integrity rather than integrity itself, we shall be the more convinced of the necessity of finding a new center of strength within ourselves.

Actually, our society has not yet found something to take the place of the gyroscope man's rigid rules. Riesman points out that the "outer-directed" people in our time generally are characterized by attitudes of *passivity* and *apathy*. The young people of today have by and large given up the driving ambition to excel, to be at the top; or if they do have such ambition, they regard it as a fault and are often apologetic for such a hangover from their fathers' mores. They want to be accepted by their peers even to the extent of being inconspicuous and absorbed in the group. This sociological picture is very similar in its broad lines to the picture we get in psychological work with individuals.

A decade or two ago, the emptiness which was beginning to be experienced on a fairly broad scale by the middle classes could be laughed at as the sickness of the suburbs. The clearest picture of the empty life is the suburban man, who gets up at the same hour every weekday morning, takes the same train to work in the city, performs the same task in the office, lunches at the same place, leaves the same tip for the waitress each day, comes home on the same train each night, has 2.3 children, cultivates a little garden, spends a two-week vacation at the shore every summer which he does not enjoy, goes to church every Christmas and Easter, and moves through a routine, mechanical existence year after year until he finally retires at sixty-five and very soon thereafter dies of heart failure, possibly brought on by repressed hostility. I have always had the secret suspicion, however, that he dies of boredom.

But there are indications in the present decade that emptiness and boredom have become much more serious states for many people. Not long ago, a very curious incident was reported in the New York papers. A bus driver in the Bronx simply drove away in his empty bus one day and was picked up by the police several days later in Florida. He explained that, having gotten tired of driving the same route every day, he had decided to go away on a trip. While he was being brought back it was clear from the papers that the bus company was having a hard time deciding whether or how he should be punished. By the time he arrived in the Bronx, he was a "cause célèbre," and a crowd of people who apparently had never personally known the errant bus driver were on hand to welcome him. When it was announced that the company had decided not to turn him over for legal punishment but to give him his job back again if he would promise to make no more jaunts, there was literal as well as figurative cheering in the Bronx.

Why should these solid citizens of the Bronx, living in a metropolitan section which is almost synonymous with middle-class urban conventionality, make a hero out of a man who according to their standards was an auto thief, and worse yet, failed to appear at his regular time for work? Was it not that this driver who got bored to death with simply making his appointed rounds, going around the same blocks and stopping at the same corners day after day, typified some similar emptiness and futility in these middle-class people, and that his gesture, ineffectual as it was, represented some deep but repressed need in the solid citizens of the Bronx? On a small scale this reminds us of the fact that the upper middle classes in bourgeois France several decades ago, as Paul Tillich has remarked, were able to endure the stultifying and mechanical routine of their commercial and industrial activities only by virtue of the presence of centers of Bohemianism at their elbows. People who live as "hollow men" can endure the monotony only by an occasional blowoff—or at least by identifying with someone else's blowoff.

In some circles emptiness is even made a goal to be sought after, under the guise of being "adaptable." Nowhere is this illustrated more arrestingly than in an article in *Life* Magazine entitled "The Wife Problem."* Summarizing a series of researches which first appeared in *Fortune* about the role of the wives of corporation executives, this article points out that whether or not the husband is promoted depends a great deal on whether his wife fits the "pattern." Time was when only the minister's wife was looked over by the trustees of the church before her husband was hired; now the wife of the corporation executive is screened, covertly or overtly, by most companies like the steel or wool or any other commodity the company uses. She must be highly gregarious, not intellectual or conspicuous, and she must have very "sensitive antennae" (again that radar set!) so that she can be forever adapting.

The "good wife is good by *not* doing things—by *not* complaining when her husband works late, by *not* fussing when a transfer is coming up; by *not* engaging in any controversial activity." Thus her success depends not on how she actively uses her powers, but on her knowing when and how to be passive. But the rule that transcends all others, says *Life*, is "*Don't be too good.* Keeping up with the Joneses is still important. But where in pushier and more primitive times it implied going substantially ahead of the Joneses, today keeping up

* January 7, 1952.

means just that: keeping up. One can move ahead, yes—but slightly, and the timing must be exquisite." In the end the company conditions almost everything the wife does—from the companions she is permitted to have down to the car she drives and what and how much she drinks and reads. To be sure, in return for this indenture the modern corporation "takes care of" its members in the form of giving them added security, insurance, planned vacations, and so on. *Life* remarks that the "Company" has become like "Big Brother"—the symbol for the dictator—in Orwell's novel, *1984*.

The editors of *Fortune* confess that they find these results "a little frightening. Conformity, it would appear, is being elevated into something akin to a religion. . . . Perhaps Americans will arrive at an ant society, not through fiat of a dictator, but through unbridled desire to get along with one another. . . ."

While one might laugh at the meaningless boredom of people a decade or two ago, the emptiness has for many now moved from the state of boredom to a state of futility and despair which holds promise of dangers. The widespread drug addiction among high-school students in New York City has been quite accurately related to the fact that great numbers of these adolescents have very little to look forward to except the army and unsettled economic conditions, and are without positive, constructive goals. The human being cannot live in a condition of emptiness for very long: if he is not growing *toward* something, he does not merely stagnate; the pent-up potentialities turn into morbidity and despair, and eventually into destructive activities.

What is the psychological origin of this experience of emptiness? The *feeling* of emptiness or vacuity which we have observed sociologically and individually should not be taken to mean that people *are* empty, or without emotional potentiality. A human being is not empty in a static sense, as though he were a storage battery which needs charging. The experience of emptiness, rather, generally comes from people's feeling that they are *powerless* to do anything effective about their lives or the world they live in. Inner vacuousness is the long-term, accumulated result of a person's particular conviction toward himself, namely his conviction that he cannot act as an entity in directing his own life, or change other people's attitudes toward him, or effectually influence the world around him. Thus he gets the deep sense of despair and futility which so many people in our day have. And soon, since what he wants and what he feels can make no real difference, he gives up wanting and feeling. Apathy and lack of feeling are also defenses against anxiety. When a person continually faces dangers he is powerless to overcome, his final line of defense is at last to avoid even feeling the dangers.

Sensitive students of our time have seen these developments coming. Erich Fromm has pointed out that people today no longer live under the authority of church or moral laws, but under "anonymous authorities" like public opinion. The authority is the public itself, but this public is merely a collection of many individuals each with his radar set adjusted to finding out what the others expect of him. The corporation executive, in the *Life* article, is at the top because he—and his wife—have been successful in "adjusting to" public opinion. The public is thus made up of all the Toms, Marys, Dicks and Harrys who are slaves to the authority of public opinion! Riesman makes the very relevant point that the public is therefore afraid of a ghost, a bogeyman, a chimera. It is an anonymous authority with a capital "A" when the authority is a composite of ourselves, but ourselves without any individual centers. We are in the long run afraid of our own collective emptiness.

And we have good reason, as do the editors of *Fortune*, to be frightened by this situation of conformity and individual emptiness. We need only remind ourselves that the ethical and emotional emptiness in European society two and three decades ago was an open invitation to fascist dictatorships to step in and fill the vacuum.

The great danger of this situation of vacuity and powerlessness is that it leads sooner or later to painful anxiety and despair, and ultimately, if it is not corrected, to futility and the blocking off of the most precious qualities of the human being. Its end results are the dwarfing and impoverishment of persons psychologically, or else surrender to some destructive authoritarianism.

Loneliness

Another characteristic of modern people is loneliness. They describe this feeling as one of being "on the outside," isolated, or, if they are sophisticated, they say that they feel alienated. They emphasize how crucial it is for them to be invited to this party or that dinner, not because they especially want to go (though they generally do go) nor because they will get enjoyment, companionship, sharing of experience and human warmth in the gathering (very often they do not, but are simply bored). Rather, being invited is crucial because it is a proof that they are not alone. Loneliness is such an omnipotent and painful threat to many persons that they have little conception of the positive values of solitude, and even at times are very frightened at the prospect of being alone. Many people suffer from "the fear of finding oneself alone," remarks André Gide, "and so they don't find themselves at all."

The feelings of emptiness and loneliness go together. When persons, for example, are telling of a break-up in a love relationship, they will often not say they feel sorrow or humiliation over a lost conquest; but rather that they feel "emptied." The loss of the other leaves an inner "yawning void," as one person put it.

The reasons for the close relation between loneliness and emptiness are not difficult to discover. For when a person does not know with any inner conviction what he wants or what he feels; when, in a period of traumatic change, he becomes aware of the fact that the conventional desires and goals he has been taught to follow no longer bring him any security or give him any sense of direction, when, that is, he feels an inner void while he stands amid the outer confusion of upheaval in his society, he senses danger; and his natural reaction is to look around for other people. They, he hopes, will give him some sense of direction, or at least some comfort in the knowledge that he is not alone in his fright. Emptiness and loneliness are thus two phases of the same basic experience of anxiety.

Perhaps the reader can recall the anxiety which swept over us like a tidal wave when the first atom bomb exploded over Hiroshima, when we sensed our grave danger—sensed, that is, that we might be the last generation—but did not know in which direction to turn. At that moment the reaction of great numbers of people was, strangely enough, a sudden, deep loneliness. Norman Cousins, endeavoring in his essay *Modern Man Is Obsolete* to express the deepest feelings of intelligent people at that staggering historical moment, wrote not about how to protect one's self from atomic radiation, or how to meet political problems, or the tragedy of man's self-destruction. Instead his editorial was a meditation on loneliness. "All man's history," he proclaimed, "is an endeavor to shatter his loneliness."

Feelings of loneliness occur when one feels empty and afraid not simply because one wants to be protected by the crowd, as a wild animal is protected by being in a pack. Nor is the longing for others simply an endeavor to fill the void within one's self—though this certainly is one side of the need for human companionship when one feels empty or anxious. The more basic reason is that the human being gets his original experiences of being a self out of his related-ness to other persons, and when he is alone, without other persons, he is afraid he will lose this experience of being a self. Man, the bio-social mammal, not only is dependent on other human beings such as his father and mother for his security during a long childhood; he likewise receives his consciousness of himself, which is the basis of his capacity to orient himself in life, from these early relationships. These important points we will discuss more thoroughly in a later chapter—here we wish only to point out that part of the feeling of loneliness is that man needs relations with other people in order to orient himself.

But another important reason for the feeling of loneliness arises from the fact that our society lays such a great emphasis on being socially accepted. It is our chief way of allaying anxiety, and our chief mark of prestige. Thus we always have to prove we are a "social success" by being forever sought after and by never being alone. If one is well-liked, that is, socially successful—so the idea goes—one will rarely be alone; not to be liked is to have lost out in the race. In the days of the gyroscope man and earlier, the chief criterion of prestige was financial success: now the belief is that if one is well-liked, financial success and prestige will follow. "Be well-liked," Willie Loman in *Death of a Salesman* advises his sons, "and you will never want."

The reverse side of modern man's loneliness is his great fear of being alone. In our culture it is permissible to say you are lonely, for that is a way of admitting that it is not good to be alone. The melancholy romantic songs present this sentiment, with the appropriate nostalgia:

> Me and my shadow,
> Not a soul to tell our troubles to . . .
> Just me and my shadow,
> All alone and feeling blue.*

And it is permissible to want to be alone temporarily to "get away from it all." But if one mentioned at a party that he liked to be alone, not for a rest or an escape, but for its own joys, people would think that something was vaguely wrong with him—that some pariah aura of untouchability or sickness hovered round him. And if a person is alone very much of the time, people tend to think of him as a failure, for it is inconceivable to them that he would choose to be alone.

This fear of being alone lies behind the great need of people in our society to get invited places, or if they invite someone else, to have the other accept. The pressure to keep "dated up" goes way beyond such realistic motives as the pleasure and warmth people get in each other's company, the enrichment of feelings, ideas and experiences, or the sheer pleasure of relaxation. Actually, such motives have very little to do with the compulsion to get invited. Many of the more sophisticated persons are well aware of these points, and would like to be able to say "No"; but they very much want the *chance* to go, and to turn down invitations in the usual round of social life means sooner or later one won't get invited. The cold fear that protrudes its icy head from subterranean levels is that one would then be shut out entirely, left on the outside.

Me and My Shadow, by Billy Rose, Al Jolson and Dave Dreyer. Copyright 1927, by Bourne, Inc., New York, N.Y., used by permission of the copyright owners.

To be sure, in all ages people have been afraid of loneliness and have tried to escape it. Pascal in the seventeenth century observed the great efforts people make to divert themselves, and he opined that the purpose of the bulk of these diversions was to enable people to avoid thoughts of themselves. Kierkegaard a hundred years ago wrote that in his age "one does everything possible by way of diversions and the Janizary music of loud-voiced enterprises to keep lonely thoughts away, just as in the forests of America they keep away wild beasts by torches, by yells, by the sound of cymbals." But the difference in our day is that the fear of loneliness is much more extensive, and the defenses against it—diversions, social rounds, and "being liked"—are more rigid and compulsive.

Let us paint an impressionistic picture of a somewhat extreme though not otherwise unusual example of the fear of loneliness in our society as seen in the social activities at summer resorts. Let us take a typical, averagely well-to-do summer colony on the seashore, where people are vacationing and therefore do not have their work available for the time being as escape and support. It is of crucial importance for these people to keep up the continual merry-go-round of cocktail parties, despite the fact that they meet the same people every day at the parties, drink the same cocktails, and talk of the same subjects or lack of subjects. What is important is not what is said, but that some talk be continually going on. Silence is the great crime, for silence is lonely and frightening. One shouldn't feel much, nor put much meaning into what one says: what you say seems to have more effect if you don't try to understand. One has the strange impression that these people are all afraid of something—what is it? It is as if the "yatata" were a primitive tribal ceremony, a witch dance calculated to appease some god. There is a god, or rather a demon, they are trying to appease: it is the specter of loneliness which hovers outside like the fog drifting in from the sea. One will have to meet this specter's leering terror for the first half-hour one is awake in the morning anyway, so let one do everything possible to keep it away now. Figuratively speaking, it is the specter of death they are trying to appease—death as the symbol of ultimate separation, aloneness, isolation from other human beings.

Admittedly, the above illustration is extreme. In the day-to-day experience of most of us, the fear of being alone may not crop up in intense form very often. We generally have methods of "keeping lonely thoughts away," and our anxiety may appear only in occasional dreams of fright which we try to forget as soon as possible in the morning. But these differences in intensity of the fear of loneliness, and the relative success of our defenses against it, do not change the central issue. Our fear of loneliness may not be shown by anxiety as such, but by subtle thoughts which pop up to remind us, when we discover we were not invited to so-and-so's party, that someone else likes us even if the person in question doesn't, or to tell us that we were successful or popular in such-and-such other time in the past. Often this reassuring process is so automatic that we are not aware of it in itself, but only of the ensuing comfort to our self-esteem. If we as citizens of the middle twentieth century look honestly into ourselves, that is, look below our customary pretenses, do we not find this fear of isolation as an almost constant companion, despite its many masquerades?

The fear of being alone derives much of its terror from our anxiety lest we *lose our awareness of ourselves*. If people contemplate being alone for longish periods of time, without anyone to talk to or any radio to eject noise into the air, they generally are afraid that they would be at "loose ends," would lose the boundaries for themselves, would have nothing to bump up against, nothing by which to orient themselves. It is interesting that they sometimes say that if they were alone for long they wouldn't be able to work or play in order to get tired; and so they wouldn't be able to sleep. And then, though they generally cannot explain this, they would lose the distinction between wakefulness and sleep, just as they lose the distinction between the subjective self and the objective world around them.

Every human being gets much of his sense of his own reality out of what others say to him and think about him. But many modern people have gone so far in their dependence on others for their feeling of reality that they are afraid that without it they would lose the sense of their own existence. They feel they would be "dispersed," like water flowing every which way on the sand. Many people are like blind men feeling their way along in life only by means of touching a succession of other people.

In its extreme form, this fear of losing one's orientation is the fear of psychosis. When persons actually are on the brink of psychosis, they often have an urgent need to seek out some contact with other human beings. This is sound, for such relating gives them a bridge to reality.

But the point we are discussing here has a different origin. Modern Western man, trained through four centuries of emphasis on rationality, uniformity, and mechanics, has consistently endeavored, with unfortunate success, to repress the aspects of himself which do not fit these uniform and mechanical standards. Is it not too much to say that modern man, sensing his own inner hollowness, is afraid that if he should not have his regular associates around him, should not have the talisman of his daily program and his routine of work, if he should forget what time it is, that he would feel, though in an inarticulate way, some threat like that which one experiences on the brink of psychosis? When one's customary ways of orienting oneself are threatened, and one is without other selves around one, one is thrown back on inner resources and inner strength, and this is what modern people have neglected to develop. Hence loneliness is a real, not imaginary, threat to many of them.

Social acceptance, "being liked," has so much power because it holds the feelings of loneliness at bay. A person is surrounded with comfortable warmth; he is merged in the group. He is reabsorbed—as though, in the extreme psychoanalytic symbol, he were to go back into the womb. He temporarily loses his loneliness; but it is at the price of giving up his existence as an identity in his own right. And he renounces the one thing which would get him constructively over the loneliness in the long run, namely the developing of his own inner resources, strength and sense of direction, and using this as a basis for meaningful relations with others. The "stuffed men" are bound to become more lonely no matter how much they "lean together"; for hollow people do not have a base from which to learn to love.

Anxiety and the Threat to the Self

Anxiety, the other characteristic of modern man, is even more basic than emptiness and loneliness. For being "hollow" and lonely would not bother us except that it makes us prey to that peculiar psychological pain and turmoil called anxiety.

No one who reads the morning newspaper needs to be persuaded that we live in an age of anxiety. Two world wars in thirty-five years, economic upheavals and depressions, the eruption of fascist barbarism and the rise of communist totalitarianism, and now not only interminable half-wars but the prospects of cold wars for decades to come while we skate literally on the edge of a Third World War complete with atom bombs—these simple facts from any daily journal are enough to show how the foundations of our world are shaken. It is no wonder that Bertrand Russell writes that the painful thing "about our time is that those who feel certainty are stupid, and those with any imagination and understanding are filled with doubt and indecision."

I have indicated in a previous book—*The Meaning of Anxiety*—that our middle of the twentieth century is more anxiety-ridden than any period since the breakdown of the Middle Ages. Those years in the fourteenth and fifteenth centuries, when Europe was inundated with anxiety in the form of fears of death, agonies of doubt about the meaning and value of life, superstition and fears of devils and sorcerers, is the nearest period comparable to our own. All one needs to do is read fears of atomic destruction where historians of that twilight of medievalism write "fears of death," loss of faith and ethical values for "agonies of doubt," and one has the beginning of a rough description of our times. We too have our superstitions in the form of anxiety about flying saucers and little men from Mars, and our "devils and sorcerers" in the demonic supermen of the Nazi and other totalitarian mythologies. Those who wish more detailed evidence of modern anxiety—as it shows itself in the rising incidence of emotional and mental disturbances, divorce and suicide, and in political and economic upheavals—can find it in the book mentioned above.

Indeed, the phrase "age of anxiety" is almost a platitude already.

We have become so inured to living in a state of quasi-anxiety that our real danger is the temptation to hide our eyes in ostrich fashion. We shall live amid upheavals, clashes, wars and rumors of wars for two or three decades to come, and the challenge to the person of "imagination and understanding" is that he face these upheavals openly, and see if, by courage and insight, he can use his anxiety constructively.

It is a mistake to believe that the contemporary wars and depressions and political threats are the total cause of our anxiety, for our anxiety also causes these catastrophes. The anxiety prevalent in our day and the succession of economic and political catastrophes our world has been going through *are both symptoms of the same underlying cause,* namely the traumatic changes occurring in Western society. Fascist and Nazi totalitarianism, for example, do not occur because a Hitler or Mussolini decides to seize power. When a nation, rather, is prey to insupportable economic want and is psychologically and spiritually empty, totalitarianism comes in to fill the vacuum; and the people sell their freedom as a necessity for getting rid of the anxiety which is too great for them to bear any longer.

The confusion and bewilderment in our nation show this anxiety on a broad scale. In this period of wars and threats of wars, we know what we are against, namely, totalitarian encroachment on man's freedom and dignity. We are confident enough of our military strength, but we fight defensively; we are like a strong animal at bay, turning this way and that, not being sure whether to fight on this flank or the other, whether to wait or to attack. As a nation we have had great difficulty deciding how far to go in Korea, whether we should make war here or there, or whether we should draw the line against totalitarianism at this point or that. If anyone should attack us, we should be completely united. But we are confused about constructive goals—what are we working *for* except defense? And even the gestures of new goals which give magnificent promise for a new world, such as the Marshall Plan, are questioned by some groups.

When an individual suffers anxiety continuously over a period of time, he lays his body open to psychosomatic illness. When a group suffers continuous anxiety, with no agreed-on constructive steps to take, its members sooner or later turn against each other. Just so, when our nation is in confusion and bewilderment, we lay ourselves open to such poison as the character assassinations of McCarthyism, witch hunts, and the ubiquitous pressures to make every man suspicious of his neighbor.

Turning our glance from the society to the individual, we see the most obvious expressions of anxiety in the prevalence of neurosis and other emotional disturbances—which, as practically everyone from Freud onward has agreed, have their root cause in anxiety. Anxiety likewise is the common denominator psychologically of the psychosomatic disturbances—such as ulcers, many of the forms of heart trouble, and so forth. Anxiety, in fine, is our modern form of the great white plague—the greatest destroyer of human health and well-being.

When we look below the surface of our individual anxiety, we find that it also comes from something more profound than the threat of war and economic uncertainty. We are anxious because we do not know what roles to pursue, what principles for action to believe in. Our individual anxiety, somewhat like that of the nation, is a basic confusion and bewilderment about where we are going. Shall a man strive competitively to become economically successful and wealthy, as we used to be taught, or a good fellow who is liked by everyone? He cannot be both. Shall he follow the supposed teaching of the society with regard to sex and be monogamous, or should he follow the average of "what's done" as shown in the Kinsey report?

These are only two examples of a condition that will be inquired into later in this book, namely the basic bewilderment about goals and values which modern people feel. Dr. and Mrs. Lynd, in their study of an American town in the middle west in the 1930's, *Middletown in Transition*, reported that the citizens of this typical community were "caught in a chaos of conflicting patterns, none of them wholly condemned, but no one of them clearly approved and free from confusion." The chief difference between Middletown in the 1930's and our present situation, I believe, is that the confusion has now gone deeper to the levels of feelings and desires. In such bewilderment many persons experience the inward gnawing apprehension of the young man in Auden's poem, *The Age of Anxiety,*

> . . . It is getting late.
> Shall we ever be asked for? Are we simply
> Not wanted at all?

If anyone believes there are simple answers to these questions, he has neither understood the questions nor the times in which we live. This is a time, as Herman Hesse puts it, "when a whole generation is caught . . . between two ages, two modes of life, with the consequence that it loses all power to understand itself and has no standards, no security, no simple acquiescence."

But it is well to remind ourselves that anxiety signifies a conflict, and so long as a conflict is going on, a constructive solution is possible. Indeed, our present upsets are as much a proof of new possibilities for the future, as we shall see below, as they are of present catastrophe. What is necessary for the constructive use of anxiety is, first of all, that we frankly admit and face our perilous state, individually and socially. As an aid to doing this, we shall now endeavor to get a clearer idea of the meaning of anxiety.

What Is Anxiety?

How shall we define anxiety, and how is it related to fear?

If you are walking across a highway and see a car speeding toward you, your heart beats faster, you focus your eyes on the distance between the car and you, and how far you have to go to get to the safe side of the road, and you hurry across. You felt fear, and it energized you to rush to safety. But if, when you start to hurry across the road, you are surprised by cars coming down the far lane from the opposite direction, you suddenly are caught in the middle of the road not knowing which way to turn. Your heart pounds faster, but now, in contrast to the experience of fear above, you feel panicky and your vision may be suddenly blurred. You have an impulse—which, let us hopefully assume, you control—to run blindly in any direction. After the cars have sped by, you may be aware of a slight faintness and a feeling of hollowness in the pit of the stomach. This is anxiety.

In fear we know what threatens us, we are energized by the situation, our perceptions are sharper, and we take steps to run or in the other appropriate ways to overcome the danger. In anxiety, however, we are threatened without knowing what steps to take to meet the danger. Anxiety is the feeling of being "caught," "overwhelmed"; and instead of becoming sharper, our perceptions generally become blurred or vague.

Anxiety may occur in slight or great intensity. It may be a mild tension before meeting some important person; or it may be apprehension before an examination when one's future is at stake and one is uncertain whether one is prepared to pass the exam. Or it may be the stark terror, when beads of sweat appear on one's forehead, in waiting to hear whether a loved one is lost in a plane wreck, or whether one's child is drowned or gets back safely after the storm on the lake. People experience anxiety in all sorts of ways: a "gnawing" within, a constriction of the chest, a general bewilderment; or they may describe it as feeling as though all the world around were dark gray or black, or as though a heavy weight were upon them, or as a feeling like the terror which a small child experiences when he realizes he is lost.

Indeed, anxiety may take all forms and intensities, for it is the human being's basic *reaction to a danger to his existence, or to some value he identifies with his existence.* Fear is a threat to one side of the self—if a child is in a fight, he may get hurt, but that hurt would not be a threat to his existence; or the university student may be somewhat scared by a midterm, but he knows the sky will not fall in if he does not pass it. But as soon as the threat becomes great enough to involve the total self, one then has the experience of anxiety. Anxiety strikes us at the very "core" of ourselves: it is what we feel when our existence as selves is threatened.

It is the quality of an experience which makes it anxiety rather than the quantity. One may feel only a slight gnawing away in one's stomach when a supposed friend passes one on the street and does not speak, but though the threat is not intense, the fact that the gnawing continues, and that one is confused and searches around for an "explanation" of why the friend snubbed one, shows the threat is to something basic in us. In its full-blown intensity, anxiety is the most painful emotion to which the human animal is heir. "Present dangers are less than future imaginings," as Shakespeare puts it; and people have been known to leap out of a lifeboat and drown rather than face the greater agony of continual doubt and uncertainty, never knowing whether they will be rescued or not.

The threat of death is the most common symbol for anxiety, but most of us in our "civilized" era do not find ourselves looking into the barrel of a gun or in other ways specifically threatened with death very often. The great bulk of our anxiety comes when some value we hold essential to our existence as selves is threatened. Tom, the man who will go down in scientific history because he had a hole in his stomach through which the doctors at New York Hospital could observe his psychosomatic reactions in times of anxiety, fear and other stress, gave a beautiful illustration of this. In a period when Tom was anxious about whether he could keep his job at the hospital or would have to go on relief, he exclaimed, "If I could not support my family, I'd as soon jump off the dock." That is, if the value of being a self-respecting wage-earner were threatened, Tom, like the salesman Willie Loman and countless other men in our society, would feel he no longer existed as a self, and might as well be dead.

This illustrates what is true in one way or another for practically all human beings. Certain values, be they success or the love of someone, or freedom to speak the truth as in the case of Socrates, or Joan of Arc's being true to her "inner voices," are believed in as the "core" of the person's reason for living, and if such a value is destroyed, the person feels his existence as a self might as well be destroyed likewise. "Give me liberty or give me death" is not just rhetoric nor is it pathological. Since the dominant values for most people in our society are being liked, accepted and approved of, much anxiety in our day comes from the threat of not being liked, being isolated, lonely or cast off.

Most examples of anxiety given above are "normal anxiety," that is, anxiety which is proportionate to the real threat of the danger situation. In a fire, battle, or crucial examination in the university, for example, anyone would feel more or less anxiety—it would be unrealistic not to. Every human being experiences normal anxiety in many different ways as he develops and confronts the various crises of life. The more he is able to face and move through these "normal crises"—the weaning from mother, going off to school, and sooner or later taking responsibility for his own vocation and marriage decisions—the less neurotic anxiety he will develop. Normal anxiety cannot be avoided; it should be frankly admitted to one's self. This book will be chiefly concerned with the normal anxiety of the person living in our age of transition, and the constructive ways this anxiety can be met.

But of course much anxiety is neurotic, and we should at least define it. Suppose a young man, a musician, goes out on his first date, and for reasons he cannot understand he is very much afraid of the girl and has a fairly miserable time. Then suppose he dodges this real problem by vowing to cut girls out of his life and devote himself only to his music. A few years later, as a successful bachelor musician, however, he finds he is very strangely inhibited around women, cannot speak to them without blushing, is afraid of his secretary, and scared to death of the women chairmen of committees he must deal with in arranging his concert schedule. He can find no objective reason for being so frightened, for he knows the women are not going to shoot him, and in actual fact have very little power over him. He is experiencing neurotic anxiety,—that is, anxiety disproportionate to the real danger, and arising from an unconscious conflict within himself. The reader already will have suspected that this young musician must have had some serious conflict with his own mother, which now carries over unconsciously and makes him afraid of all women.

Most neurotic anxiety comes from such unconscious psychological conflicts. The person feels threatened, but it is as though by a ghost; he does not know where the enemy is, or how to fight it or flee from it. These unconscious conflicts usually get started in some previous situation of threat which the person did not feel strong enough to face, such as a child's having to deal with a dominating and possessive parent or having to face the fact that his parents don't love him. The real problem is then repressed, and it returns later as an inner conflict bringing with it neurotic anxiety. The way to deal with neurotic anxiety is to bring out the original real experience one was afraid of, and then to work the apprehension through as normal anxiety or fear. In dealing with any severe neurotic anxiety, the mature and wise step is to get professional psychotherapeutic help.

But our main concern in these chapters is to understand how to use normal anxiety constructively. And to do that we need to make clearer one very important point, the relation between a person's anxiety and his self-awareness. After a terrifying experience such as a battle or fire, people often remark, "I felt as though I were in a daze." This is because anxiety knocks out the props, so to speak, from our awareness of ourselves. Anxiety, like a torpedo, strikes underneath at the deepest level, or "core," of ourselves, and it is on this level that we experience ourselves as persons, as subjects who can act in a world of objects. Thus anxiety in greater or lesser degree tends to destroy our consciousness of ourselves. In a battle, for example, so long as the enemy attacks the front lines, the soldiers in the defending army, despite their fear, continue fighting. But if the enemy succeeds in blowing up the center of communications behind the lines, then the army loses its direction, the troops move helter-skelter, and the army is no longer aware of itself as a fighting unit. The soldiers are then in a state of anxiety, or panic. This is what anxiety does to the human being: it disorients him, wiping out temporarily his clear knowledge of what and who he is, and blurring his view of reality around him.

This bewilderment—this confusion as to who we are and what we should do—is the most painful thing about anxiety. But the positive and hopeful side is that just as anxiety destroys our self-awareness, so awareness of ourselves can destroy anxiety. That is to say, the stronger our consciousness of ourselves, the more we can take a stand against and overcome anxiety. Anxiety, like fever, is a sign that an inner struggle is in progress. As fever is a symptom that the body is mobilizing its physical powers and giving battle to the infection, let us say the tuberculosis bacilli in the lungs, so anxiety is evidence that a psychological or spiritual battle is going on. We have noted above that neurotic anxiety is the sign of an unresolved conflict within us, and so long as the conflict is present, there is an open possibility that we can become aware of the causes of the conflict, and find a solution on a higher level of health. Neurotic anxiety is nature's way, as it were, of indicating to us that we need to solve a problem. The same is true of normal anxiety—it is a signal for us to call up our reserves and do battle against a threat.

As the fever in our example is a symptom of the battle between the bodily powers and the infecting germs, so anxiety is evidence of a battle between our strength as a self on one side and a danger which threatens to wipe out our existence as a self on the other. The more the threat wins, the more then our awareness of ourselves is surrendered, curtailed, hemmed in. But the greater our self-strength—that is, the greater our capacity to preserve our awareness of ourselves and the objective world around us—the less we will be overcome by the threat. There is still hope for a tuberculous patient so long as he has fever; but in the final stages of the disease, when the body has "given up" as it were, the fever leaves and soon the patient dies. Just so, the only thing which would signify the loss of hope for getting through our present difficulties as individuals and as a nation, would be a resigning into apathy, and a failure to feel and face our anxiety constructively.

Our task, then, is to strengthen our consciousness of ourselves, to find centers of strength within ourselves which will enable us to stand despite the confusion and bewilderment around us. This is the central purpose of the inquiry in this book. First, however, we shall endeavor to see more clearly how our present predicament came upon us.

2

The Roots of Our Malady

⁕

THE first step in overcoming problems is to understand their causes. What has been happening in our Western World that individuals and nations should be buffeted about by so much confusion and bewilderment? Let us first ask—with a brief glance into our historical background—what basic changes are occurring which make this an age of anxiety and emptiness?

The Loss of the Center of Values in Our Society

The central fact is that we live at one of those points in history when one way of living is in its death throes, and another is being born. That is to say, the values and goals of Western society are in a state of transition. What, specifically, are the values that we have lost?

One of the two central beliefs in the modern period since the Renaissance has been in the value of individual competition. The conviction was that the more a man worked to further his own economic self-interest and to become wealthy, the more he would contribute to the material progress of the community. This famous laissez-faire theory in economics worked well for several centuries. It *was* true through the early and growing stages of modern industrialism and capitalism that for you or me to strive to become rich by increasing our trade or building a bigger factory would eventually mean the production of more material goods for the community. The pursuit of competitive enterprise was a magnificent and courageous idea in its heyday. But in the nineteenth and twentieth centuries considerable changes occurred. In our present day of giant business and monopoly capitalism how many people can become successful as *individual* competitors? There are very few groups left who, like doctors and psychotherapists and some farmers, still have the luxury of being their own economic bosses—and even they are subject to the rise and fall of prices and the fluctuating market like everyone else. The vast majority of workingmen and capitalists alike, professional people or businessmen, must fit into broad groups such as labor unions or big industries or university systems, or they would not survive economically at all. We have been taught to strive to get ahead of the next man, but actually today one's success depends much more on how well one learns to work with one's fellow workers. I have just read that even the individual crook cannot make out very well on his own these days: he has to join a racket!

We do not mean that something is wrong with individual effort and initiative as such. Indeed, the chief argument of this book is that the unique powers and initiative of each individual must be rediscovered, and used as a basis for work which contributes to the good of the community, rather than melted down in the collectivist pot of conformity.

But we do mean that in the twentieth century, when scientific and other advances have made us much more closely interdependent in our nation as well as in our world, individualism must become a different thing from "each man for himself and the devil take the hindmost." If you or I had a farm to carve out of the frontier forest two centuries ago, or possessed a little capital with which to start a new business last century, the philosophy of "each man for himself" would have brought out the best in us and resulted in the best for the community. But how does such competitive individualism work in a day when even corporation wives are screened to fit the "pattern"?

The individual's striving for his own gain, in fine, without an equal emphasis on social welfare, no longer automatically brings good to the community. Furthermore, this type of individual competitiveness—in which for you to fail in a deal is as good as for me to succeed, since it pushes me ahead in the scramble up the ladder—raises many psychological problems. It makes every man the potential enemy of his neighbor, it generates much interpersonal hostility and resentment, and increases greatly our anxiety and isolation from each other. As this hostility has come closer to the surface in recent decades, we have tried to cover it up by various devices—by becoming "joiners" of all sorts of service organizations, from Rotary to Optimist Clubs in the 1920's and 30's, by being good fellows, well liked by all, and so on. But the conflicts sooner or later burst forth into the open.

This is pictured beautifully and tragically in Willie Loman, the chief character in Arthur Miller's *Death of a Salesman*. Willie had been taught, and in turn taught his sons, that to get ahead of the next fellow and to get rich were the goals, and this required initiative. When the boys steal balls and lumber, Willie, though he pays lip-service to the idea that he should rebuke them, is pleased that they are "fearless characters" and remarks that the "coach will probably congratulate them on their initiative." His friend reminds him that the jails are full of "fearless characters," but Willie rejoins, "the stock exchange is too."

Willie tries to cover up his competitiveness, like most men of two or three decades ago, by being "well liked." When as an old man he is "cast into the ash can" by virtue of the changing policies of his company, Willie is caught in great bewilderment, and keeps repeating to himself, "But I was the best-liked." His confusion in this conflict of values—why does what he was taught not work?—mounts up until it culminates in his suicide. At the grave one son continues to insist, "He had a good dream, to come out number one." But the other son accurately sees the contradiction which such an upheaval of values leads to, "He never knew who he was."*

The second central belief in our modern age has been the faith in individual reason. This belief, ushered in at the Renaissance like the belief in the value of individual competitiveness which we have just been discussing, was magnificently fruitful for the philosophical

* *Death of a Salesman,* by Arthur Miller, New York, Viking Press, 1949.

quests of the enlightenment in the seventeenth century, and served as a noble charter for the advances in science and for movements toward universal education. In these first centuries of our period, individual reason also meant "universal reason"; it was a challenge to each intelligent person to discover the universal principles by which all men might live happily.

But again a change became apparent in the nineteenth century. Psychologically, reason became separated from "emotion" and "will." The splitting up of the personality was prepared by Descartes in his famous dichotomy between body and mind—which will dog our tracks throughout this book—but the full consequences of this dichotomy did not emerge till last century. For the late nineteenth- and early twentieth-century man, reason was supposed to give the answer to any problem, will power was supposed to put it into effect, and emotions—well, they generally got in the way, and could best be repressed. Lo and behold, we then find reason (now transformed into intellectualistic rationalization) used in the service of compartmentalizing the personality, with the resulting repressions and conflict between instinct and ego and superego which Freud so well described. When Spinoza in the seventeenth century used the word reason, he meant an attitude toward life in which the mind united the emotions with the ethical goals and other aspects of the "whole man." When people today use the term they almost always imply a splitting of the personality. They ask in one form or another: "Should I follow reason *or* give way to sensual passions and needs *or* be faithful to my ethical duty?"

The beliefs in individual competition and reason we have been discussing are the ones which in *actuality* have guided modern western development, and are not necessarily the ideal values. To be sure, the values accepted as *ideal* by most people have been those of the Hebrew-Christian tradition allied with ethical humanism, consisting of such precepts as love thy neighbor, serve the community, and so on. On the whole, these ideal values have been taught in schools and churches hand in hand with the emphasis on competition and individual reason. (We can see the watered-down influence of the values of "service" and "love" coming out in roundabout fashion in the "service clubs" and the great emphasis on being "well liked.") Indeed, the two sets of values—the one running back many centuries to the sources of our ethical and religious traditions in ancient Palestine and Greece and the other born in the Renaissance—were to a considerable extent wedded. For example, Protestantism, which was the religious side of the cultural revolution beginning in the Renaissance, expressed the new individualism by emphasizing each person's right and ability to find religious truth for himself.

The marriage had a good deal to be said for it, and for several centuries the squabbles between the marriage partners were ironed out fairly well. For the ideal of the brotherhood of man *was* to a considerable extent furthered by economic competition—the tremendous scientific gains, the new factories and the more rapid moving of the wheels of industry increased man's material weal and physical health immensely, and for the first time in history our factories and our science can now produce so much that it is possible to wipe starvation and material want from the face of the earth. One could well have argued that science and competitive industry were bringing mankind ever closer to its ethical ideals of universal brotherhood.

But in the last few decades it has become clear that this marriage is full of conflict, and is headed for drastic overhauling or for divorce. For now the great emphasis on one person getting ahead of the other, whether it be getting higher grades in school, or more stars after one's name in Sunday school, or gaining proof of salvation by being economically successful, greatly blocks the possibilities of loving one's neighbor. And, as we shall see later, it even blocks the love between brother and sister and husband and wife in the same family. Furthermore, since our world is now made literally "one world" by scientific and industrial advances, our inherited emphasis on individual competitiveness is as obsolete as though each man were to deliver his own letters by his own pony express. The final eruption which showed the underlying contradictions in our society was fascist totalitarianism, in which the humanist and Hebrew-Christian values, particularly the value of the person, were flouted in a mammoth upsurgence of barbarism.

Some readers may be thinking that many of the above questions are stated wrongly—why does economic striving need to be *against* one's fellow men, and why reason *against* emotion? True, but the characteristic of a period of change like the present is precisely that everyone does ask the wrong questions. The old goals, criteria, principles are still there in our minds and "habits," but they do not fit, and hence most people are eternally frustrated by asking questions which never could lead to the right answer. Or they become lost in a potpourri of contradictory answers—"reason" operates while one goes to class, "emotion" when one visits one's lover, "will power" when one studies for an exam, and religious duty at funerals and on Easter Sunday. This compartmentalization of values and goals leads very quickly to an undermining of the unity of the personality, and the person, in "pieces" within as well as without, does not know which way to go.

Several great men living in the last of the nineteenth and first of the twentieth century saw the splitting up of personality which was occurring. Henrik Ibsen in literature realized what was happening, Paul Cézanne in art, and Sigmund Freud in the science of human nature. Each of these men proclaimed that we must find a new unity for our lives. Ibsen showed in his play *A Doll's House* that if the husband simply goes off to business, keeping his work and his family in different compartments like a good nineteenth-century banker, and treats his wife as a doll, the house will collapse. Cézanne attacked the artificial and sentimental art of the nineteenth century and showed that art must deal with the honest realities of life, and that beauty has more to do with integrity than with prettiness. Freud pointed out that if people repress their emotions and try to act as if sex and anger did not exist, they end up neurotic. And he worked out a new technique for bringing out the deeper, unconscious, "irrational" levels in personality which had been suppressed, thus helping the person to become a thinking-feeling-willing unity.

So significant was the work of Ibsen, Cézanne and Freud that many of us used to believe that they were the prophets for our times. True, the contribution of each is probably the most important in their respective fields. But were they not in one respect the last great men of the old period rather than the first of the new? For they presupposed the values and goals of the past three centuries; important and enduring as their new techniques were, they coasted on the goals of their time. They lived before the age of emptiness.

It seems now, unfortunately, that the true prophets for the middle twentieth century were Soren Kierkegaard, Friedrich Nietzsche, and Franz Kafka. I say "unfortunately" because that means our task is that much more difficult. Each one of these men foresaw the destruction of values which would occur in our time, the loneliness, emptiness and anxiety which would engulf us in the twentieth century. Each saw that we cannot ride on the goals of the past. We shall quote these three frequently in this book, not because they are intrinsically the wisest men in history, but because each foresaw with great power and insight the particular dilemmas which almost every intelligent person faces now.

Friedrich Nietzsche, for example, proclaimed that science in the late nineteenth century was becoming a factory, and he feared that man's great advances in techniques without a parallel advance in ethics and self-understanding would lead to nihilism. Uttering prophetic warnings about what would happen in the twentieth century, he wrote a parable about the "death of God." It is a haunting story of a madman who runs into the village square shouting, "Where is God?" The people around did not believe in God; they laughed and said perhaps God had gone on a voyage or emigrated. The madman then shouted: "Whither is God?"

> "I shall tell you! We have killed him—you and I! . . . yet how have we done this? . . . Who gave us the sponge to wipe away the whole horizon? What did we do when we unchained this earth from its sun? . . . Whither do we move now? Away from all suns? Do we not fall incessantly? Backward, sideward, forward, in all directions? Is there yet any up and down? Do we not err as through an infinite naught? Do we not feel the breath of empty space? Has it not become colder? Is not night and more night coming on all the while? . . . God

is dead! God remains dead! . . . and we have killed him! . . ." Here the madman became silent and looked again at his listeners: They too remained silent and looked at him. . . ."I come too early," he said then. . . ."This tremendous event is still on its way."*

Nietzsche is not calling for a return to the conventional belief in God, but he is pointing out what happens when a society loses its center of values. That his prophecy came true is shown in the waves of massacres, pogroms and tyranny in the middle twentieth century. The tremendous event *was* on its way; a frightful night of barbarism did descend on us when the humanistic and Hebrew-Christian values of our period were so flouted.

The way out, says Nietzsche, is a finding of a center of values anew—what he terms "revaluation" or "transvaluation" of all values. *"Revaluation of all values,"* he proclaims, "that is my formula for an act of ultimate self-examination by mankind."†

The upshot is that the values and goals which provided a unifying center for previous centuries in the modern period no longer are cogent. We have not yet found the new center which will enable us to choose our goals constructively, and thus to overcome the painful bewilderment and anxiety of not knowing which way to move.

The Loss of the Sense of Self

Another root of our malady is our loss of the sense of the worth and dignity of the human being. Nietzsche predicted this when he pointed out that the individual was being swallowed up in the herd, and that we were living by a "slave-morality." Marx also predicted it when he proclaimed that modern man was being "de-humanized," and Kafka showed in his amazing stories how people literally can lose their identity as persons.

* Quoted from *Nietzsche*, by W. Kaufmann, Princeton Univ. Press, 1950, p. 75.
† *Ibid.*, p. 89.

But this loss of the sense of self did not occur overnight. Those of us who lived in the 1920's can recall the evidences of the growing tendency to think of the self in superficial and oversimplified terms. In those days "self-expression" was supposed to be simply doing whatever popped into one's head, as though the self were synonymous with any random impulse, and as though one's decisions were to be made on the basis of a whim which might be a product of indigestion from a hurried lunch just as often as of one's philosophy of life. To "be yourself" was then an excuse for relaxing into the lowest common denominator of inclination. To "know one's self" wasn't thought to be especially difficult, and the problems of personality could be solved relatively easily by better "adjustment." These views were furthered by oversimplified psychology like John B. Watson's brand of behaviorism. We were then congratulating ourselves that the child could be conditioned out of fear, superstition and other problems by techniques not essentially different from the way the dog's saliva is conditioned to flow every time the dinner gong rings. These superficial views of the human situation were also furthered by the belief in automatic economic progress—we would all get richer and richer without too much struggle or suffering. And these views got their final sanction in a religious moralism flourishing in the 1920's which had never developed beyond the Sunday-school stage, and smacked more of Couéism and Pollyannaism than of the profound insights of the historical ethical and religious leaders. Practically everyone who put pen to paper in those days shared the same oversimplified view of the human being: Bertrand Russell (who, I believe, would take a quite different view today) wrote in the 1920's that science was advancing so rapidly that soon we would give people whatever temperament one desired, choleric or timid, strongly or weakly sexed, merely by chemical injections into the body. This kind of push-button psychology was due for the satire which Aldous Huxley gave it in his *Brave New World*.

Though the 1920's seemed to be a time when men had great confidence in the power of the person, it was actually the opposite: they had confidence in techniques and gadgets, not in the human being.

The oversimplified, mechanical view of the self really betokened an underlying lack of belief in the dignity, complexity and freedom of the person.

In the two decades since the 1920's, the disbelief in the power and dignity of the person became more openly accepted, for there appeared a good deal of concrete "evidence" that the individual self was insignificant and that one's personal choices didn't matter. In the face of totalitarian movements and uncontrolled economic earthquakes like the major depression, we tended to feel smaller and smaller as persons. The individual self was dwarfed into as ineffectual a position as the proverbial grain of sand pushed around by ocean breakers:

> We move on
> As the wheel wills; one revolution
> Registers all things, the rise and fall
> In pay and prices.*

Most people now, therefore, are able to find good external "reasons" for their belief that as selves they are insignificant and powerless. For how can one act, they well ask, in the face of the giant economic, political and social movements of the time? Authoritarianism in religion and science, let alone politics, is becoming increasingly accepted, not particularly because so many people explicitly believe in it but because they feel themselves individually powerless and anxious. So what else can one do, goes the reasoning, except follow the mass political leader (as happened in Europe) or follow the authority of customs, public opinion, and social expectations as is the tendency in this country?

What is forgotten in such "reasoning," is, of course, the fact that the loss of belief in the worth of the person is partly the *cause* of these mass social and political movements. Or, to put it more accurately, the loss of the self and the rise of collectivist movements, as we have pointed out, are both the result of the same underlying historical

---

*W. H. Auden, *The Age of Anxiety*, p. 45, New York, Random House.

changes in our society. We need, therefore, to fight on both flanks—to oppose totalitarianism and the other tendencies toward dehumanization of the person on one flank, and to recover our experience and belief in the worth and dignity of the person on the other.

A startling picture of the loss of the sense of self in our society is given in a short novel, *The Stranger*, by the contemporary French author Albert Camus. It is the story of a Frenchman who is extraordinary in no respect—indeed, he might well be called an "average" modern man. He experiences the death of his mother, goes to work and about the ordinary things of life, has an affair and sexual experiences, all without any clear decision or awareness on his part. He later shoots a man, and it is vague even in his own mind whether he shot by accident or in self-defense. He goes through a murder trial and is executed, all with a horrible sense of unreality, as though everything happened *to* him: he never acted himself. The book is pervaded by a vagueness and haze which is frustrating and shocking, like the similar haze of indecisiveness in Kafka's stories. Everything seems to take place in a dream, with the man never really related to the world or anything he does or to himself. He is a man without courage or despair, despite the outwardly tragic events, because he has no awareness of himself. At the end when he is awaiting execution he almost gets a glimmer of the realization, as expressed, say in the words of George Herbert,

> A sick toss'd vessel, dashing on each thing . . .
> My God, I mean myself.

Almost, but not quite; there is not enough sense of himself for even that to break through. The novel is a haunting and subtly terrifying picture of the modern man who is truly a "stranger" to himself.

Less dramatic illustrations of the loss of the sense of power of the self are present all around us in contemporary society, and, indeed, are so common that we generally take them for granted. For example, there is the curious remark made regularly nowadays at the end of radio programs, "Thanks for listening." This remark is quite amazing when you come to think of it. Why should the person who is doing the entertaining, who is *giving* something ostensibly of value, thank the receiver for taking it? To acknowledge applause is one thing, but thanking the recipient for deigning to listen and be amused is a quite different thing. It betokens that the action is given its value, or lack of value, by the whim of the consumer, the receiver—in the case of our illustration the consumers being their majesties, the public. Imagine Kreisler, after playing a concerto, thanking the audience for listening! The parallel suggested by the radio announcer's remark is the court jester, who not only had to perform but at the same time to beg the majesties who watched to deign to be amused—and proverbially the court jester was in as humiliating a position as a human being could occupy.

Obviously we are not criticizing radio announcers as such. This remark merely illustrates an attitude which runs through our society: so many people judge the value of their actions not on the basis of the action itself, but on the basis of how the action is accepted. It is as though one had always to postpone his judgment until he looked at his audience. The person who is passive, to whom or for whom the act is done, has the power to make the act effective or ineffective, rather than the one who is doing it. Thus we tend to be *performers* in life rather than persons who live and act as selves.

To use an illustration from the sphere of sex, it is as though a man were to perform intercourse in the attitude of imploring the woman to "please be satisfied"—an attitude which actually exists, though often unconsciously, among men in our society more widely than is generally realized. And, to illustrate how this attitude backfires in personal relations, we may add that if the man is mainly concerned with satisfying the woman, his full abandon and active strength do not come into the relationship, and in many cases this is precisely the reason the woman does not receive full gratification. No matter how skillful the gigolo's technique, what woman would choose it as a substitute for the reality of passion? The essence of the gigolo, court-jester attitude is that power and value are correlated not with action but with passivity.

Another example of how the sense of the self has been disintegrating in our day can be seen when we consider humor and laughter. It is not generally realized how closely one's sense of humor is connected with one's sense of selfhood. Humor normally should have the function of preserving the sense of self. It is an expression of our uniquely human capacity to experience ourselves as subjects who are not swallowed up in the objective situation. It is the healthy way of feeling a "distance" between one's self and the problem, a way of standing off and looking at one's problem with perspective. One cannot laugh when in an anxiety panic, for then one is swallowed up, one has lost the distinction between himself as subject and the objective world around him. So long as one can laugh, furthermore, he is not completely under the domination of anxiety or fear—hence the accepted belief in folklore that to be able to laugh in times of danger is a sign of courage. In cases of borderline psychotics, so long as the person has genuine humor—so long, that is, as he can laugh, or look at himself with the thought, as one person put it, "What a crazy person I've been!"—he is preserving his identity as a self. When any of us, neurotic or not, get insights into our psychological problems, our spontaneous reaction is normally a little laugh—the "aha" of insight, as it is called. The humor occurs because of a new appreciation of one's self as a subject acting in an objective world.

Now having seen the function humor normally fills for the human being, let us ask, What are the prevalent attitudes toward humor and laughter in our society? The most striking fact is that laughter is made a commodity. We speak of "a laugh," or one remarks that a movie or radio program has "such and such number of laughs" as shown by a computing and volume-recording machine, as though laughter was a quantity like a dozen oranges or a bushel of apples.

To be sure, there are some exceptions—the writings of E. B. White, for a rare example, show how humor can deepen the reader's feeling of worth and dignity as a person, and remove blinds from his eyes as he confronts the issues facing him. But in general humor and laughter in our day mean "laughs" in quantitative form, produced by mail-order, push-button techniques, as is the case, let us say, of the productions of the gag writers for the radio. Indeed, the term "gag" is a fitting one: the "laughs" serve as "laughing gas," in Thorstein Veblen's vivid phrase, to furnish a dulling of sensitivities and awareness just as gas does in actuality. Laughter is then an escape from anxiety and emptiness in ostrich-fashion rather than a way of gaining new and more courageous perspective in facing one's perplexities. Such laughter, which is often expressed in the raucous guffaw, may have the function of a simple release of tension, like alcohol or sexual stimulation; but, again like sex or drinking when engaged in for escapist reasons, this kind of laughter leaves one as lonely and unrelated to himself afterwards as before. Some laughter, of course, is of the vindictive type. This is the laugh of triumph, the telltale mark of which is that the laughter bears no relation to smiling. One may thus laugh in anger or rage. It often seemed to me that this was the kind of grimace one saw on the face of Hitler in the photographs in which he was supposed to be "smiling." Vindictive laughter goes along with seeing one's self as triumphant over other selves, rather than being an indication of a new step in the achievement of one's own selfhood. Vindictive laughter, as well as the quantitative laughter of the "laughing gas" variety, reflects the humor of people who have to a great extent lost the sense of the dignity and significance of persons.

The loss of the sense of the significance and worth of the self, indeed, will be one of the major stumbling blocks for some readers in following the discussion throughout this book. Many persons, sophisticated as often as unsophisticated ones, have lost their conviction of how crucially important the problem of rediscovering the sense of self is. They still assume that "being one's self" means only what "self-expression" meant in the 1920's, and they may then ask (with some justification on the basis of their assumptions), "Would not being one's self be both unethical and boring?" and "Does one have to express one's self in playing Chopin?" Such questions themselves are evidence of how far the profound meaning of being one's self has been lost. Thus many people in our day find it almost impossible to realize that Socrates, in his precept "know thyself," was urging upon the individual the most difficult challenge of all. And they likewise find it almost impossible to understand what Kierkegaard meant when he proclaimed, "To venture in the highest sense is precisely to become conscious of one's self . . ."

The Loss of Our Language for Personal Communication

Along with the loss of the sense of self has gone a loss of our language for communicating deeply personal meanings to each other. This is one important side of the loneliness now experienced by people in the Western world. Take the word "love" for example, a word which obviously should be most important in conveying personal feelings. When you use it, the person you are talking to may think you mean Hollywood love, or the sentimental emotion of the popular songs, "I love my baby, my baby loves me," or religious charity, or friendliness, or sexual impulse, or whatnot. The same is true about almost any other important word in the nontechnical areas—"truth," "integrity," "courage," "spirit," "freedom," and even the word "self." Most people have private connotations for such words which may be quite different from their neighbor's meaning, and hence some people even try to avoid using such words.

We have an excellent vocabulary for technical subjects, as Erich Fromm has pointed out; almost every man can name the parts of an automobile engine clearly and definitely. But when it comes to meaningful interpersonal relations, our language is lost: we stumble, and are practically as isolated as deaf and dumb people who can only communicate in sign language. As Eliot has his "hollow men" phrase it,

> Our dried voices, when
> We whisper together
> Are quiet and meaningless
> As wind in dry grass
> Or rats' feet over broken glass
> In our dry cellar.*

* "The Hollow Men," in *Collected Poems*, New York, Harcourt, Brace and Co., 1934, p. 101.

This loss of the effectiveness of language, it may seem strange to point out, is a symptom of a disrupted historical period. When you explore the rise and fall of historical eras, you will note how the language is powerful and compelling at certain times, like the Greek language of the fifth century B.C. in which Aeschylus and Sophocles wrote their classics, or like the Elizabethan English of Shakespeare and the King James translation of the Bible. At other periods the language is weak, vague and uncompelling, such as when Greek culture was being disrupted and dispersed in the Hellenistic period. I believe it could be shown in researches—which obviously cannot be gone into here—that when a culture is in its historical phase of growing toward unity, its language reflects the unity and power; whereas when a culture is in the process of change, dispersal and disintegration, the language likewise loses its power.

"When I was eighteen, Germany was eighteen," said Goethe, referring not only to the fact that the ideals of his nation were then moving toward unity and power, but that the language, which was his vehicle of power as a writer, was also in that stage. In our day the study of semantics is of considerable value, to be sure, and is to be commended. But the disturbing question is why we have to talk so much about what words mean that, once we have learned each other's language, we have little time or energy left for communicating.

There are other forms of personal communication than words: art and music, for example. Painting and music are the voices of the sensitive spokesmen in the society communicating deeply personal meanings to others in the society, as well as to other societies and other historical periods. Again, we find in modern art and modern music a language which does not communicate. If most people, even intelligent ones, look at modern art without knowing the esoteric key, they can understand practically nothing. They are greeted by every kind of style—impressionism, expressionism, cubism, abstractionism, representationalism, nonobjective painting, until Mondrian gives his message only in squares and rectangles, and Jackson Pollock, in a kind of *reductio ad absurdum*, spatters paint in almost accidental forms on large boards and entitles the work simply the date on which it was completed. I of course imply no criticism of these artists, both of whom happen to give me pleasure. But does it not imply something very significant about our society that talented artists can communicate only in such limited language?

If you visit the Art Students League in New York—which has perhaps the largest group of outstanding American artists as teachers and the most representative body of students—you will be surprised to find the classes in practically every studio painting in a distinctly different style, and you will have to shift emotional gears every twenty steps. In the Renaissance a common man could look at the paintings of Raphael or Leonardo da Vinci or Michelangelo and feel that the picture was telling him something which he could understand about life in general and his own inner life in particular. But if an untutored man walked through the galleries on 57th Street in New York City today and saw, let us say, exhibits by Picasso, Dali and Marin, he might well agree that something important was being communicated but he would no doubt aver that only God and the artist knew what it was. For his own part he would probably be bewildered, and possibly somewhat irritated.

Nietzsche said a person is to be known by his "style," that is, by the unique "pattern" which gives underlying unity and distinctiveness to his activities. The same is partly true about a culture. But when we ask what is the "style" of our day, we find that there is no style which can be called modern. The one thing these many modern different movements in art have in common, beginning with the great work of Cézanne and Van Gogh, is that they all are trying desperately to break through the hypocrisy and sentimentality of nineteenth-century art. Consciously or unconsciously, they seek to speak in their painting from some solid reality in the self experiencing the world. But beyond this desperate search for honesty, which is much like that of Freud and Ibsen in their respective fields, there is only a potpourri of styles. Making all necessary qualifications for the fact that time has not yet done its sifting for the modern period as it has, say, for the Renaissance, it is still true that this potpourri is a revealing picture of the disunity of our times. The pictures that are discordant and empty, as are so many in modern art, are thus honest portrayals of the condition of our time.

It is as though every genuine artist were frantically trying different languages to see which one would communicate the music of form and color to his fellow men, but there is no common language. We find a giant like Picasso shifting in his own lifetime from style to style, partly as a reflection of the shifting character of the last four decades in Western society, and partly like a man dialing a ship's radio on the ocean, trying vainly to find the wave length on which he can talk to his fellow men. But the artists, and the rest of us too, remain spiritually isolated and at sea, and so we cover up our loneliness by chattering with other people about the things we do have language for—the world series, business affairs, the latest news reports. Our deeper emotional experiences are pushed further away, and we tend, thus, to become emptier and lonelier.

"Little We See in Nature That Is Ours"

People who have lost the sense of their identity as selves also tend to lose their sense of relatedness to nature. They lose not only their experience of organic connection with inanimate nature, such as trees and mountains, but they also lose some of their capacity to feel empathy for animate nature, that is animals. In psychotherapy, persons who feel empty are often sufficiently aware of what a vital response to nature might be to know what they are missing. They may remark, regretfully, that though others are moved by a sunset, they themselves are left relatively cold; and though others may find the ocean majestic and awesome, they themselves, standing on rocks at the seashore, don't feel much of anything.

Our relation to nature tends to be destroyed not only by our emptiness, but also by our anxiety. A little girl coming home from school after a lecture on how to defend one's self against the atom bomb, asked her parent, "Mother, can't we move someplace where there isn't any sky?" Fortunately this child's terrifying but revealing question is an allegory more than an illustration, but it well symbolizes how anxiety makes us withdraw from nature. Modern man, so afraid of the bombs he has built, must cower from the sky and hide in caves—must cower from the sky which is classically the symbol of vastness, imagination, release.

On a more everyday level, our point is simply that when a person feels himself inwardly empty, as is the case with so many modern people, he experiences nature around him also as empty, dried up, dead. The two experiences of emptiness are two sides of the same state of impoverished relation to life.

We can see more clearly what it means to lose one's feeling for nature if we glance back to note how the sense of relationship to nature flourished in the modern period, and then died down. One of the chief characteristics of the Renaissance in Europe was an upsurging of enthusiasm for nature in all its forms—whether in the form of animals, or of trees, or in the inanimate form of stars and colors in the sky. One can see this new feeling coming beautifully to life in the paintings of Giotto in the early Renaissance. If, after looking at the stylized and stiff forms of nature in medieval art, you suddenly come upon the frescoes of Giotto, you will be surprised by the most charming sheep, lively dogs and winsome donkeys, all presented as vital parts of human experience. And you will likewise be surprised to see that Giotto, in contrast to the artists of the Middle Ages, paints rocks and trees as natural forms delightful for their own beauty, not simply for their symbolic religious message; and that, also in contrast to medieval art, he shows human beings experiencing joy, grief, contentment as *individual* emotions. His paintings tell us more powerfully than words that when a human being experiences himself as an identity who actively *feels* his relation to life as an individual, he also experiences an alive relation to animals and nature.

The new appreciation of nature was also shown in the Renaissance enthusiasm for the human body. One can see this in many forms: in the sensuality in Boccaccio's stories, in the heroically powerful and harmonious bodies in Michelangelo's paintings, and in the feeling for the physical as part of the many-sided, organic approach to life in Shakespeare's dramas. It was shown, furthermore, in the new enthusiasm for the scientific study of nature. One aspect, thus, of the strength of these towering individuals of the Renaissance—those "universal men"—was their strong feeling for nature.

But by the nineteenth century the interest in nature had become increasingly technical; man's concern now was chiefly to *master and manipulate* nature. The world had become "disenchanted" in Paul Tillich's colorful phrase. To be sure, the disenchantment process had begun way back in the seventeenth century, when Descartes taught that the body and mind were to be separated, that the objective world of physical nature and the body (which could be measured and weighed) was radically different from the subjective world of man's mind and "inner" experience. The practical result of this dichotomy was that subjective, "inner" experience—the "mind" side of the dichotomy—tended to be put on the shelf, and modern man had a heyday pursuing, with great success, the mechanical, measurable aspects of experience. So by the nineteenth century nature had largely become impersonal, as in science, or an object to be calculated for the purpose of making money, as the geographer charts the seas for the purposes of commerce.

Obviously, when we point out that the overemphasis on things which could be calculated and manipulated went hand in hand with the growth of industrialism and bourgeois commerce, we are implying no criticism of machines and technical progress as such. We mean simply to point out the historical fact that in this development nature became separated from the individual's subjective, emotional life.

Near the beginning of the nineteenth century William Wordsworth, among others, clearly saw this loss of the feeling for nature, and he saw the overemphasis on commercialism which was partly its cause and the emptiness which would be its result. He described what was occurring in his familiar sonnet:

The world is too much with us; late and soon,
Getting and spending, we lay waste our powers:
Little we see in Nature that is ours;
We have given our hearts away, a sordid boon!
This Sea that bares her bosom to the moon,

The winds that will be howling at all hours,
And are up-gather'd now like sleeping flowers;
For this, for everything, we are out of tune;
It moves us not.—Great God! I'd rather be
A Pagan suckled in a creed outworn;
So might I, standing on this pleasant lea,
Have glimpses that would make me less forlorn;
Have sight of Proteus rising from the sea;
Or hear old Triton blow his wreathèd horn.

It is not by poetic accident that Wordsworth yearns for such mythological creatures as Proteus and Triton. These figures are personifications of aspects of nature—Proteus, the god who keeps changing his shape and form, is a symbol for the sea which is eternally transforming its movement and its color. Triton is the god whose horn is the sea shell, and his music is the echoing hum one hears in the large shells on the shore. Proteus and Triton are examples of precisely what we have lost—namely the capacity to see ourselves and our moods in nature, to relate to nature as a broad and rich dimension of our own experience.

Descartes' dichotomy had given modern man a philosophical basis for getting rid of the belief in witches, and this contributed considerably to the actual overcoming of witchcraft in the eighteenth century. Everyone would agree that this was a great gain. But we likewise got rid of the fairies, elves, trolls, and all of the demicreatures of the woods and earth. It is generally assumed that this, too, was a gain since it helped sweep man's mind clean of "superstition" and "magic." But I believe this is an error. Actually what we did in getting rid of the fairies and the elves and their ilk was to impoverish our lives; and impoverishment is not the lasting way to clear men's minds of superstition. There is a sound truth in the old parable of the man who swept the evil spirit out of his house, but the spirit, noticing that the house stood clean and vacant, returned bringing seven more evil spirits with him; and the second state of the man was worse than the first. For it is the empty and vacant people who seize on the new and more destructive forms of our latter-day superstitions, such as beliefs in the totalitarian mythologies, engrams, miracles like the day the sun stood still, and so on. Our world has become disenchanted; and it leaves us not only out of tune with nature but with ourselves as well.

As human beings we have our roots in nature, not simply because of the fact that the chemistry of our bodies is of essentially the same elements as the air or dirt or grass. In a multitude of other ways we participate in nature—the rhythm of the change of seasons or of night and day, for example, is reflected in the rhythm of our bodies, of hunger and fulfillment, of sleep and wakefulness, of sexual desire and gratification, and in countless other ways. Proteus can be a personification of the changes in the sea because he symbolizes what we and the sea share—changing moods, variety, capriciousness, and adaptability. In this sense, when we relate to nature we are but putting our roots back into their native soil.

But in another respect man is very different from the rest of nature. He possesses consciousness of himself; his sense of personal identity distinguishes him from the rest of the living or nonliving things. And nature cares not a fig for man's personal identity. That crucial point in our relatedness to nature brings into the center of the picture the basic theme of this book, man's need for awareness of himself. One must be able to affirm his person despite the impersonality of nature, and to fill the silences of nature with his own inner aliveness.

It takes a strong self—that is, a strong sense of personal identity— to relate fully to nature without being swallowed up. For really to feel the silence and the inorganic character of nature carries a considerable threat. If one stands on a rocky promontory, for example, and looks at the sea in its tremendous rising and falling of swells, and if one is fully and realistically aware that the sea never "has a tear for others' woes nor cares what any other thinks," that one's life could be swallowed up with scarcely an infinitesimal difference being made to the tremendous, ongoing, chemical movement of creation, one is threatened. Or if one gives himself to the feeling of the distance of the far mountain peaks, permits himself to "empathize" with their heights and depths, and if one is aware at the same moment that the mountain "never was the friend of one, nor promised what it could not give," and that one could be dashed to pieces on the stone floor at the foot of the peak without his extinction as a person making the slightest difference to the walls of granite, one is afraid. This is the profound threat of "nothingness," or "nonbeing," which one experiences when he fully confronts his relation with inorganic being. And to remind one's self, "Dust thou art, to dust returnest" is hollow comfort indeed.

Such experiences in relating to nature have too much anxiety for most people. They flee from the threat by shutting off their imagination, by turning their thoughts to the practical and humdrum details of what to have for lunch. Or they protect themselves from the full terror of the threat of nonbeing by making the sea a "person" who wouldn't hurt them, or by taking refuge in some belief in individual Providence and telling themselves, "He shall give his angels charge concerning thee . . . lest at any time thou dash thy foot against a stone." But to flee from one's anxiety, or to rationalize one's way out of it, only makes one weaker in the long run.

It requires, we have said, a strong sense of self and a good deal of courage to relate to nature creatively. But to affirm one's own identity over against the inorganic being of nature in turn produces greater strength of self. At this point, however, we are getting ahead of our story—how such strength is developed belongs to the discussion in later chapters. We wish here only to emphasize that the loss of the relation to nature goes hand in hand with the loss of the sense of one's own self. "Little we see in Nature that is ours," as a description of many modern people, is a mark of the weakened and impoverished person.

The Loss of the Sense of Tragedy

A final consequence and evidence of the loss of our conviction of the worth and dignity of the person is that we have lost the sense of the tragic significance of human life. For the sense of tragedy is simply the other side of one's belief in the importance of the human individual. Tragedy implies a profound respect for the human being and a devotion to his rights and destiny—otherwise it just doesn't matter whether Orestes or Lear or you or I fall or stand in our struggles.

Arthur Miller, in the preface to his play *The Death of a Salesman*, makes some telling comments on the lack of tragedy in our day. The tragic character, he writes, is one "who is ready to lay down his life, if need be, to secure one thing—his sense of personal dignity." And "the tragic right is a condition of life, a condition in which the human personality is able to flower and realize itself." These conditions obtained in the periods in Western history when great tragedy was written. One has only to look at fifth-century Greece, when Aeschylus and Sophocles wrote the mighty tragedies of Oedipus, Agamemnon and Orestes, or at Elizabethan England when Shakespeare gave us Lear and Hamlet and Macbeth.

But in our age of emptiness, tragedies are relatively rare. Or if they are written, the tragic aspect is the very fact that human life is so empty, as in Eugene O'Neill's drama, *The Iceman Cometh*. This play is set in a saloon, and its dramatis personae—alcoholics, prostitutes, and, as the chief character, a man who in the course of the play goes psychotic—can dimly recall the periods in their lives when they did believe in something. It is this echo of human dignity in a great void of emptiness that gives this drama the power to elicit the emotions of pity and terror of classical tragedy.

Arthur Miller's *Death of a Salesman*, which we have mentioned earlier, is itself one of the few real tragedies about the common people—neither alcoholics nor psychotics—who make up the social situation in this country out of which most of us have sprung. (In the movie version of this drama, Willie Loman, the salesman, is unfortunately made to look pathetic—those who saw only the movie may have to imagine Willie in a broader context to appreciate his real tragic import.) He was a man who took seriously the teachings of his society, that success should attend hard, energetic work, that economic progress is a reality and that if one has the right "contacts" achievement and salvation should follow. It is easy enough from our later perspective to see through Willie's illusions, and to poke fun at his unsound go-getter values. But that is not the point. The one thing that matters is that Willie *believed*; he took seriously his own existence and what he had been taught he could rightly expect from life. "I don't say he is a great man," says his wife in describing Willie's disintegration to their sons, "but he's a human being, and a terrible thing is happening to him. So attention must be paid." The tragic fact is not that Willie is a man of the grandeur of Lear or the inward richness of Hamlet; "he's only a little boat looking for a harbor," as his wife also says. But it is the tragedy of a historical period—if one multiplies Willie by the hundreds of thousands of fathers and brothers who also believed what they were taught but found in the changing times that it did not work, one has enough to shake one with pity and fear as in the tragedies of old. "He never knew who he was," and he was one who took seriously his right to know.

"The flaw, or crack in the tragic character," Miller writes, "is really nothing—and need be nothing—but his inherent unwillingness to remain passive in the face of what he conceives to be a challenge to his dignity, his image of his rightful status. Only the passive, only those who accept their lot without active retaliation, are 'flawless.' Most of us are in that category." Miller goes on to point out that the quality in a tragedy which shakes us "derives from the underlying fear of being displaced, the disaster inherent in being torn away from our chosen image of what and who we are in this world. Among us today this fear is as strong, and perhaps stronger, than it ever was."*

Let no one assume we are advocating a pessimistic view when we mourn the loss of the tragic sense. On the contrary, as Miller also notes, "Tragedy implies more optimism in its author than does comedy, and . . . its final result ought to be the reinforcement of the onlooker's brightest opinions of the human animal." For the tragic view indicates that we take seriously man's freedom and his need to realize himself; it demonstrates our belief in the "indestructible will of man to achieve his humanity."

* *Op. cit.*, Preface.

The knowledge of human nature and the insights into man's unconscious conflicts which are disclosed in psychotherapy give new ground for believing in the tragic aspects of human life. The psychotherapist, privileged to be an intimate witness to some persons' inner wrestling and their often grave and bitter struggles with themselves and with external forces which challenge their dignity, gains a new respect for these persons and a new realization of the potential dignity of the human being. Countless times a week, furthermore, he receives proof in his consulting work that when men at last accept the fact that they cannot successfully lie to themselves, and at last learn to take themselves seriously, they discover previously unknown and often remarkable recuperative powers within themselves.

THE PICTURE of the roots of the malady of our time given in this chapter adds up to a bleak diagnosis. But it does not necessarily imply a bleak prognosis. For the positive side is that we have no choice but to move ahead. We are like people part way through psychoanalysis whose defenses and illusions are broken through, and their only choice is to push on to something better.

We—and by we I mean everyone, however old or young, who is aware of the historical situation in which we live—are not the "lost" generation of the 1920's. The term "lost," when applied to members of that period of adolescent rebellion following the first World War, meant that one was temporarily away from home, and could go back again whenever one became too frightened at being on one's own. But we are, rather, the generation which cannot turn back. We in the middle of the twentieth century are like pilots in the transatlantic flight who have passed the point of no return, who do not have fuel enough to go back but must push on regardless of storms or other dangers.

What, then, is the task before us? The implications are clear in the above analysis: we must rediscover the sources of strength and integrity within ourselves. This, of course, goes hand in hand with the discovery and affirmation of values in ourselves and in our society which will serve as the core of unity. But no values are effective, in a person or a society, except as there exists in the person the prior capacity to do the valuing, that is, the capacity actively to choose and affirm the values by which he lives. This the individual must do, and in this way he will help lay the groundwork for the new constructive society which will eventually come out of this disturbed time, as the Renaissance came out of the disintegration of the Middle Ages.

William James once remarked that those who are concerned with making the world more healthy had best start with themselves. We could go farther and point out that finding the center of strength within ourselves is in the long run the best contribution we can make to our fellow men. It is said that when the fisherman in the sea around Norway sees his boat heading for a maelstrom, he reaches ahead to try to throw an oar into the boiling whirlpool; if he can do so, the maelstrom quiets down, and he and his boat go safely through. Just so, one person with indigenous inner strength exercises a great calming effect on panic among people around him. This is what our society needs—not new ideas and inventions, important as these are, and not geniuses and supermen, but persons who can *be*, that is, persons who have a center of strength within themselves. It is our task in these chapters to try to find the sources of this inner strength.

Part 2

✳

REDISCOVERING SELFHOOD

3

The Experience of Becoming a Person

※

To undertake this "venture of becoming aware of ourselves," and to discover the sources of inner strength and security which are the rewards of such a venture, let us start at the beginning by asking, What is this person, this sense of selfhood we seek?

A few years ago a psychologist procured a baby chimpanzee the same age as his infant son. In order to do an experiment, such as is the wont of these men, he raised the baby chimp and baby human being in his household together. For the first few months they developed at very much the same speed, playing together and showing very little difference. But after a dozen months or so, a change began to occur in the development of the little human baby, and from then on there was a great difference between him and the chimp.

This is what we would expect. For there is very little difference between the human being and any mammal baby from the time of the original unity of the foetus in the womb of its mother, through the beginning of the beating of its own heart, then its ejection as an infant from the womb at birth, the commencing of its own breathing and the first protected months of life. But around the age of two, more or less, there appears in the human being the most radical and important emergence so far in evolution, namely his consciousness of himself. He begins to be aware of himself as an "I." As the foetus in the womb, the infant has been part of the "original we" with its mother, and it continues as part of the psychological "we" in early infancy. But now the little child—for the first time—becomes aware of his freedom. He senses his freedom, as Gregory Bateson puts it, within the context of the relationship with his father and mother. He experiences himself as an identity who is separated from his parents and can stand against them if need be. This remarkable emergence is the birth of the human animal into a person.

Consciousness of Self—the Unique Mark of Man

This consciousness of self, this capacity to see one's self as though from the outside, is the distinctive characteristic of man. A friend of mine has a dog who waits at his studio door all morning and, when anybody comes to the door, he jumps up and barks, wanting to play. My friend holds that the dog is saying in his barking: "Here is a dog who has been waiting all morning for someone to come to play with him. Are you the one?" This is a nice sentiment, and all of us who like dogs enjoy projecting such cozy thoughts into their heads. But actually this is exactly what the dog cannot say. He can show that he wants to play and entice you into throwing his ball for him, but he cannot stand outside himself and see himself as a dog doing these things. He is not blessed with the consciousness of self.

Inasmuch as this means the dog is also free from neurotic anxiety and guilt feelings, which are the doubtful blessings of the human being, some people would prefer to say the dog is not *cursed* with the consciousness of self. Walt Whitman, echoing this thought, envies the animals:

> I think I could turn and live with animals. . . .
> They do not sweat and whine about their condition,
> They do not lie awake in the dark and weep for their sins . . .

But actually man's consciousness of himself is the source of his highest qualities. It underlies his ability to distinguish between "I" and the world. It gives him the capacity to keep time, which is simply the ability to stand outside the present and to imagine oneself back in yesterday or ahead in the day after tomorrow. Thus human beings can learn from the past and plan for the future. And thus man is the historical mammal in that he can stand outside and look at his history; and thereby he can influence his own development as a person, and to a minor extent he can influence the march of history in his nation and society as a whole. The capacity for consciousness of self also underlies man's ability to use symbols, which is a way of disengaging something from what it is, such as the two sounds which make up the word "table," and agreeing that these sounds will stand for a whole class of things. Thus man can think in abstractions like "beauty," "reason," and "goodness."

This capacity for consciousness of ourselves gives us the ability to see ourselves as others see us and to have empathy with others. It underlies our remarkable capacity to transport ourselves into someone else's parlor where we will be in reality next week, and then in imagination to think and plan how we will act. And it enables us to imagine ourselves in someone else's place, and to ask how we would feel and what we would do if we were this other person. No matter how poorly we use or fail to use or even abuse these capacities, they are the rudiments of our ability to begin to love our neighbor, to have ethical sensitivity, to see truth, to create beauty, to devote ourselves to ideals, and to die for them if need be.

To fulfill these potentialities is to be a person. This is what is meant when it is stated in the Hebrew-Christian religious tradition that man is created in the image of God.

But these gifts come only at a high price, the price of anxiety and inward crises. The birth of the self is no simple and easy matter. For the child now faces the frightful prospect of being out on his own, alone, and without the full protection of the decisions of his parents. It is no wonder that when he begins to feel himself an identity in his own right, he may feel terribly powerless in comparison with the great and strong adults around him. In the midst of a struggle over her dependency on her mother, one person had this eloquent dream: "I was in a little boat tied to a big boat. We were going through the ocean and big waves came up, piling over the sides of my boat. I wondered whether it was still tied to the big boat."

The healthy child, who is loved and supported but not coddled by his parents, will proceed in his development despite this anxiety and the crises that face him. And there may be no particular external signs of trauma or special rebelliousness. But when his parents consciously or unconsciously exploit him for their own ends or pleasure, or hate or reject him, so that he cannot be sure of minimal support when he tries out his new independence, the child will cling to the parents and will use his capacity for independence only in the forms of negativity and stubbornness. If, when he first begins tentatively to say "No," his parents beat him down rather than love and encourage him, he thereafter will say "No" not as a form of true independent strength but as a mere rebellion.

Or if, as in the majority of cases in the present day, the parents themselves are anxious and bewildered in the tumultuous seas of the changing times, unsure of themselves and beset by self-doubts, their anxiety will carry over and lead the child to feel that he lives in a world in which it is dangerous to venture into becoming one's self.

This brief sketch is schematic, to be sure, and it is meant to give us as adults a kind of retrospective picture in the light of which we can better understand how one fails to achieve selfhood. Most of the data for these conflicts of childhood come from adults who are struggling, in dreams, memories or in present-day relations, to overcome what in their past lives originally blocked them in becoming fully born as persons. Almost every adult is, in greater or lesser degree, still struggling on the long journey to achieve selfhood on the basis of the patterns which were set in his early experiences in the family.

Nor do we for a moment overlook the fact that selfhood is always born in a social context. Genetically, Auden is quite right:

> . . . for the ego is a dream
> Till a neighbor's need by name create it.*

Or, as we put it above, the self is always born and grows in interpersonal relationships. But no "ego" moves on into responsible selfhood

---

* *Age of Anxiety,* New York, Random House, p. 8.

if it remains chiefly the reflection of the social context around it. In our particular world in which conformity is the great destroyer of selfhood—in our society in which fitting the "pattern" tends to be accepted as the norm, and being "well liked" is the alleged ticket to salvation—what needs to be emphasized is not only the admitted fact that we are to some extent created by each other but also our capacity to experience, and create, ourselves.

On the very day I was writing these words, a young intern reported in his psychoanalytic session a dream which is essentially parallel to the dreams of almost everyone who is in a crisis in his growth. This young man had originally come for psychoanalytic help as a medical student because of attacks of anxiety so severe and prolonged that he was on the verge of dropping out of medical school. His problems were chiefly due to his close tie to his mother, a very unstable but strong and dominating woman. Having by now completed his medical studies, he was a successful intern and had applied for the most responsible residency in the hospital for the next year. The day preceding the night on which he had this dream, he had received a letter from the hospital directors awarding him the residency and paying him compliments on his excellent work as an intern. But instead of being pleased, he had been suddenly seized with an attack of anxiety. The dream follows in his own words:

> I was bicycling to my childhood home where my father and mother were. The place seemed beautiful. When I went in, I felt free and powerful, as I am in my real life as a doctor now, not as I was as a boy. But my mother and father would not recognize me. I was afraid to express my independence for fear I would be kicked out. I felt as lonely and separate as though I were at the North Pole and there were no people around but only snow and ice for thousands of miles. I walked through the house, and in the different rooms were signs tacked up, "Wipe your feet," and "Clean your hands."

The anxiety after his being offered the desired position indicates that something in it, or in the responsibility it entailed, very much frightened him. And the dream tells us why. If he is a responsible, independent person in his own right—in contrast to the boy tied to his mother's apron strings—he will be ejected from his family, and will be isolated and alone. The fascinating vignettes in the form of the "wipe-your-feet" signs add a footnote which says the house is like a military camp and not a loving home at all.

The real question facing this young man, of course, was why he dreamed of going home at all—what need was there within himself to go back to mother and father and the house he pictured as externally beautiful in the dream, when he is confronted with responsibility? This is a question we shall deal with later. Here let us only emphasize how becoming a person, an identity in one's own right, is the original development which begins in infancy and carries over into adulthood no matter how old one may be; and the crises it involves may cause tremendous anxiety. No wonder many persons repress the conflict and try all their lives to run from the anxiety!

What does it mean to experience one's self as a self? The experience of our own identity is the basic conviction that we all start with as psychological beings. It can never be proven in a logical sense, for consciousness of one's self is the presupposition of any discussion about it. There will always be an element of mystery in one's awareness of one's own being—mystery here meaning a problem the data of which encroach on the problem. For such awareness is a presupposition of inquiry into one's self. That is to say, even to meditate on one's own identity as a self means that one is already engaging in self-consciousness.

Some psychologists and philosophers are distrustful of the concept of self. They argue against it because they do not like separating man from the continuum with animals, and they believe the concept of the self gets in the way of scientific experimentation. But rejecting the concept of "self" as "unscientific" because it cannot be reduced to mathematical equations is roughly the same as the argument two and three decades ago that Freud's theories and the concept of "unconscious" motivation were "unscientific." It is a defensive and dogmatic science—and therefore not true science—which uses a particular scientific method as a Procrustean bed and rejects all forms of human experience which don't fit. To be sure, the continuum between man and animals should be seen clearly and realistically; but one need not jump to the unwarranted conclusion that therefore there is no distinction between man and animals.

We do not need to prove the self as an "object." It is only necessary that we show how people have the capacity for self-relatedness. The self is the organizing function within the individual and the function by means of which one human being can relate to another. It is prior to, not an object of, our science; it is presupposed in the fact that one can be a scientist.

Human experience always goes beyond our particular methods of understanding it at any given moment, and the best way to understand one's identity as a self is to look into one's own experience. Let us, for example, imagine the inner experience of some psychologist or philosopher writing a paper to deny the concept of consciousness of self. During the weeks he was considering writing this paper, he no doubt many times pictured himself sitting at his desk at some future day writing away. And from time to time, let us say, both before he actually began to write and later as he sat at his desk at work on the paper, he considered in fantasy what his colleagues would say about the paper, whether Professor So-and-So would praise it, whether other colleagues would say, "How brilliant this is!" whether still others might think it stupid, and so on. In every thought he is seeing himself as an identity as definitely as he would see a colleague walking across the street. His every thought in the process of arguing against the consciousness of self proves this very consciousness in himself.

The consciousness of one's identity as a self certainly is not an intellectual idea. The French philosopher Descartes, at the beginning of the modern period three centuries ago, crawled into his stove, according to legend, to meditate in solitude all one day trying to find the basic principle for human existence. He came out of his stove in the evening with the famous conclusion "I think, therefore I am." That is to say, I exist as a self because I am a thinking creature. But this is not enough. You and I never think of ourselves as an idea. We rather picture ourselves as doing something, like the psychologist writing his paper, and we then experience in imagination the feelings that we will have when we are in actuality doing that thing. That is to say, we experience ourselves as a thinking-intuiting-feeling and acting unity. The self is thus not merely the sum of the various "roles" one plays—it is the capacity by which one *knows* he plays these roles; it is the center from which one sees and is aware of these so-called different "sides" of himself.

After these perhaps high-sounding phrases, let us remind ourselves that after all the experience of one's own identity, or becoming a person, is the simplest experience in life even though at the same time the most profound. As everyone knows, a little child will react indignantly and strongly if you, in teasing, call him by the wrong name. It is as though you take away his identity—a most precious thing to him. In the Old Testament the phrase "I will blot out their names"—to erase their identity and it will be as though they never had existed—is a more powerful threat even than physical death.

Two little girl twins gave a vivid illustration of how important it is for a child to be a person in her own right. The little girls were good friends, a fact made especially possible because they complemented each other, one being extrovert and always in the center of the crowd if people came to visit in the house, the other being perfectly happy by herself to draw with her crayons and make up little poems. The parents, as parents generally do with twins, had dressed them alike when they went out walking. When they were about three and a half, the little extrovert girl began to want always to wear a different kind of dress from her sister. If she dressed after her sister, she would even, if necessary, wear an older and less pretty dress so that it would not be the same as the twin was wearing. Or if the sister dressed after her before they went out, she would beg her, sometimes weeping, not to put on the matching dress. For days this puzzled the parents, since the child was not anxious in other ways. Finally the parents, on a hunch, asked the little girl, "When you two go out walking, do you like to have the people on the street say, 'Look at these nice twins'?"

Immediately the little girl exclaimed, "No, I want them to say, 'Look at these two different people!'"

This spontaneous exclamation, obviously revealing something very important to the little girl, cannot be explained by saying that the child wanted attention; for she would have gotten more attention if she had dressed as a twin. It shows, rather, her demand to be a person in her own right, to have personal identity—a need which was more important to her even than attention or prestige.

The little girl rightly stated the goal for every human being—to become a person. Every organism has one and only one central need in life, to fulfill its own potentialities. The acorn becomes an oak, the puppy becomes a dog and makes the fond and loyal relations with its human masters which befit the dog; and this is all that is required of the oak tree and the dog. But the human being's task in fulfilling his nature is much more difficult, for he must do it in self-consciousness. That is, his development is never automatic but must be to some extent chosen and affirmed by himself. "Among the works of man," John Stuart Mill has written, "which human life is rightly employed in perfecting and in beautifying, the first importance surely is man himself. . . . Human nature is not a machine to be built after a model and set to do exactly the work prescribed for it, but a tree, which requires to grow and develop itself on all sides, according to the tendency of the inward forces which make it a living thing." In this charmingly expressed thought, John Stuart Mill has unfortunately omitted the most important "tendency of the inward forces" which make man a living thing, namely that man does not grow automatically like a tree, but fulfills his potentialities only as he in his own consciousness plans and chooses.

Fortunately the long protracted period of infancy and childhood in human life—in contrast to the condition of the acorn, which is on its own as soon as it falls to the soil, or of the puppy which must fend for itself after a few weeks—prepares the child for this difficult task. He is able to acquire some knowledge and inner strength so that as he must begin to choose and decide, he has some capability for it.

Man, furthermore, must make his choices as an individual, for individuality is one side of one's consciousness of one's self. We can see this point clearly when we realize that consciousness of one's self is always a unique act—I can never know exactly how you see yourself and you never can know exactly how I relate to myself. This is the inner sanctum where each man must stand alone. This fact makes for much of the tragedy and inescapable isolation in human life, but it also indicates again that we must find the strength in ourselves to stand in our own inner sanctum as individuals. And this fact means that, since we are not automatically merged with our fellows, we must through our own affirmation learn to love each other.

If any organism fails to fulfill its potentialities, it becomes sick, just as your legs would wither if you never walked. But the power of your legs is not all you would lose. The flowing of your blood, your heart action, your whole organism would be the weaker. And in the same way if man does not fulfill his potentialities as a person, he becomes to that extent constricted and ill. This is the essence of neurosis—the person's unused potentialities, blocked by hostile conditions in the environment (past or present) and by his own internalized conflicts, turn inward and cause morbidity. "Energy is Eternal Delight," said William Blake; "He who desires but acts not, breeds pestilence."

Kafka was a master at the gruesome task of picturing people who do not use their potentialities and therefore lose their sense of being persons. The chief character in *The Trial* and in *The Castle* has no name—he is identified only by an initial, a mute symbol of one's lack of identity in one's own right. In the staggering and frightful parable, *Metamorphosis*, Kafka illustrates what happens when the human being forfeits his powers. The hero of this story is a typical, empty modern young man, who lives a routine, vacuous life as a salesman, returning regularly to his middle-class home, eating the same menu of roast beef every Sunday while his father goes to sleep at the table. The young man's life was so empty, implies Kafka, that he woke up one morning no longer a human being but a cockroach. Because he had not fulfilled his status as a man, he forfeited his human potentialities. A cockroach, like lice and rats and vermin, lives off others' leavings. It is a parasite, and in most people's minds a symbol for what is unclean and repugnant. Could there be any more powerful symbol of what happens when a human being relinquishes his nature as a person?

But to the extent that we do fulfill our potentialities as persons, we experience the profoundest joy to which the human being is heir. When a little child is learning to walk up steps or lift a box, he will try again and again, getting up when he falls down and starting over again. And finally when he does succeed, he laughs with gratification, his expression of joy in the use of his powers. But this is nothing in comparison to the quiet joy when the adolescent can use his newly emerged power for the first time to gain a friend, or the adult's joy when he can love, plan and create. Joy is the affect which comes when we use our powers. Joy, rather than happiness, is the goal of life, for joy is the emotion which accompanies our fulfilling our natures as human beings. It is based on the experience of one's identity as a being of worth and dignity, who is able to affirm his being, if need be, against all other beings and the whole inorganic world. This power in its ideal form is shown in the life of a Socrates, who was so confident in himself and his values that he could take his being condemned to death not as a defeat but as a greater fulfillment than compromising his beliefs. But we do not wish to imply such joy is only for the heroic and the outstanding; it is as present qualitatively in anyone's act, no matter how inconspicuous, which is done as an honest and responsible expression of his own powers.

Self-Contempt, a Substitute for Self-Worth

But here we must pause to answer two objections. Some readers may be thinking that this emphasis on the necessity and value of consciousness of self will make people "too concerned" about themselves. One objection would be that it leads one to be "too introspective," and another that it makes for pride in one's self. Persons with this latter objection might raise the questions, "Are we not told not to think too highly of ourselves? And has it not been proclaimed that man's pride in himself is the root of most evil in our time?"

Let us consider the latter objection first. To be sure, one ought not to think too highly of one's self, and a courageous humility is the mark of the realistic and mature person. But thinking too highly of one's self, in the sense of self-inflation and conceit, does not come from greater consciousness of one's self or greater feelings of self-worth. In fact, it comes from just the opposite. Self-inflation and conceit are generally the external signs of inner emptiness and self-doubt; a show of pride is one of the most common covers for anxiety. Pride was a chief characteristic of the famous roaring 1920's, but we know now that this period was one of widespread, suppressed anxiety. The person who feels weak becomes a bully, the inferior person the braggart; a flexing of muscles, much talk, cockiness, an endeavor to brazen it out, are the symptoms of covert anxiety in a person or a group. Tremendous pride was exhibited in fascism, as everyone knows who has seen the pictures of the strutting Mussolini and psychopathic Hitler; but fascism is a development in people who are empty, anxious and despairing, and therefore seize on megalomaniac promises.

To push this question deeper, many of the arguments in our day against pride in one's self, and many of the homilies on alleged self-abnegation, have a motive quite other than humility or a courageous facing of one's human situation. A great number of these arguments, for example, reveal a considerable contempt for the self. Aldous Huxley writes, "For all of us, the most intolerably dreary and deadening life is that which we live with ourselves." Fortunately, it can be remarked immediately, this generalization is obviously untrue; it is empirically not a fact that the most dreary and deadening hours of Spinoza were those he lived with himself, or of Thoreau or of Einstein or of Jesus or of many a human being who has no fame whatever but who has ventured, as Kierkegaard puts it, to become conscious of himself. In fact, I seriously doubt whether Huxley's remark is true even of himself, or of Reinhold Niebuhr, or others who with so much self-confidence and assertiveness proclaim the evils of man's asserting himself. Indeed, it is very easy to get an audience these days if one preaches against conceit and pride in one's self, for most people feel so empty and convinced of their lack of worth anyway that they readily agree that the one who is condemning them must be right.

This leads us to the most important point of all in understanding the dynamics of much modern self-condemnation, namely that *condemning ourselves is the quickest way to get a substitute sense of worth*. People who have almost, but not quite, lost their feeling of worth generally have very strong needs to condemn themselves, for that is the most ready way of drowning the bitter ache of feelings of worthlessness and humiliation. It is as though the person were saying to himself, "I must be important that I am so worth condemning," or "Look how noble I am: I have such high ideals and I am so ashamed of myself that I fall short." A psychoanalyst once pointedly remarked that when someone in psychoanalysis berates himself at great length for picayune sins, he feels like asking, "Who do you think you are?" The self-condemning person is very often trying to show how important he is that God is so concerned with punishing him.

Much self-condemnation, thus, is a cloak for arrogance. Those who think they overcome pride by condemning themselves could well ponder Spinoza's remark, "One who despises himself is the nearest to a proud man." In ancient Athens when a politician was trying to get the votes of the working class by appearing very humble in a tattered coat with big holes in it, Socrates unmasked his hypocrisy by exclaiming, "Your vanity shows forth from every hole in your coat."

The mechanism of much of this self-condemnation in our day can be observed in psychological depressions. The child, for example, who feels he is not loved by his parents can always say, generally to himself, "If I were different, if I were not bad, they would love me." By this means he avoids facing the full force and the terror of the realization that he is not loved. Thus, too, with adults: if they can condemn themselves they do not need really to feel the pain of their isolation or emptiness, and the fact that they are not loved then does not cast doubt upon their feeling of worth as persons. For they can always say, "If it were not for such and such a sin or bad habit, I would be loved."

In our age of hollow people, the emphasis upon self-condemnation is like whipping a sick horse: it achieves a temporary lift, but it hastens the eventual collapse of the dignity of the person. The self-condemning substitute for self-worth provides the individual with a method of avoiding an open and honest confronting of his problems of isolation and worthlessness, and makes for a pseudo-humility rather than the honest humility of one who seeks to face his situation realistically and do what he can constructively. Furthermore, the self-condemning substitute provides the individual with a rationalization for his self-hate, and thus reinforces the tendencies toward hating himself. And, inasmuch as one's attitudes toward other selves generally parallel one's attitude toward one's self, one's covert tendency to hate others is also rationalized and reinforced. The steps are not big from the feeling of worthlessness of one's self to self-hatred to hatred for others.

In the circles where self-contempt is preached, it is of course never explained why a person should be so ill-mannered and inconsiderate as to force his company on other people if he finds it so dreary and deadening himself. And furthermore the multitude of contradictions are never adequately explained in a doctrine which advises that we should hate the one self, "I," and love all others, with the obvious expectation that they will love us, hateful creatures that we are; or that the more we hate ourselves, the more we love God who made the mistake, in an off moment, of creating this contemptible creature, "I."

Fortunately, however, we no longer have to argue that self-love is not only necessary and good but that it also is a prerequisite for loving others. Erich Fromm, in his persuasive analysis, *Selfishness and Self-love*, has made it clear that selfishness and excessive self-concern really come from an inner self-hatred. He points out that self-love is not only not the same as selfishness but is actually the *opposite* to it. That is to say, the person who inwardly feels worthless is the one who must build himself up by selfish aggrandizement, and the person who has a sound experience of his own worth, that is who loves himself, has the basis for acting generously toward his neighbor. Fortunately, it also becomes clear from a longer religious perspective that much contemporaneous self-condemning and self-contempt are a product of particular modern problems. Calvin's contemptuous view of the self was closely related to the fact that individuals felt so insignificant in the industrial developments of the modern period. And the twentieth-century self-contempt arises not only from Calvinism but also from our disease of emptiness. Thus the modern self-contemptuous emphasis is not representative of the long-term Hebrew-Christian tradition. Kierkegaard has expressed this most forcibly:

> If anyone, therefore, will not learn from Christianity to love *himself* in the right way, then neither can he love his neighbor. . . . To love one's self in the right way and to love one's neighbor are absolutely analogous concepts, are at bottom one and the same. . . . Hence the law is: "You shall love yourself as you love your neighbor when you love him as yourself."*

Consciousness of Self Is Not Introversion

The other objection we mentioned above may arise in the reader's mind in questions like these: "Ought we not to try to forget ourselves? Does not consciousness of one's self make one self-conscious in the sense of being shy, embarrassed and socially inhibited?" Some questioners would no doubt mention the famous centipede, who came to grief because of too much "thinking which leg came after which, and so lay distracted in the ditch." The moral of the centipede, obviously, is "See what happens to you if you get too conscious of what you are doing."

Before answering these objections we must point out how unfortunate it is that self-consciousness is identified in this country with morbid introspection, shyness and embarrassment. Naturally, the last thing in the world anyone would want, then, to be is self-conscious. But our language plays tricks on us. The German language is more accurate in this regard: the word for self-consciousness also means "self-confident," which is as it should be.

An example will make clear that what we are talking about is just the opposite to shyness, embarrassment and morbid introversion. A

---

* *A Kierkegaard Anthology.* Robert Bretall, ed. Princeton, 1946, p. 289.

young man came for psychotherapy because, though he was intellectually very competent and seemed superficially to be very successful, his spontaneity was almost completely blocked. He could not love anyone and he got no real enjoyment from human companionship. These problems were accompanied by a good deal of anxiety and recurrent depressions. It had always been his habit to stand outside himself, looking at himself, never letting himself go, until the self-concern became exceedingly painful. In listening to music, he was so concerned with how well he was listening that he would not hear the music. Even in making love, it was as though he were standing outside, watching himself and asking, "How am I doing?" As could be imagined, this put quite a crimp in his style. He was afraid, when he entered psychotherapy and discovered that he would have to become more aware of what was going on within himself, that he would become more "self-conscious" and therefore his problems would become worse.

He was the only child of anxious parents who had very much overprotected him, never going out at night, for example, because of their hesitancy to leave him alone. Though the parents were ostensibly "liberal" and "rational" in all dealings with the son, he could never remember in all his childhood that he ever once talked back to them. The parents would brag about his achievements in school to relatives, cutting clippings about his successes from the papers and taking pride in the fact that he was brighter than his cousins: but they rarely expressed real appreciation directly to him. Thus already as a child he was unable to develop a feeling of his own independent power and worth, and used as a substitute an overconcern for the praise which came, at least indirectly, from winning prizes in school. Add to this that he spent his early teens in Hitler Germany, where he was exposed continuously to propaganda about his supposed worthlessness as a Jew. Thus his standing off and continually looking at himself as an adult was like continuing to cut clippings from the paper, judging and measuring himself, trying to prove to himself that the Nazis were not right, and trying to get genuine affirmation of himself as a person from his parents. This case is very much oversimplified, to be sure. We wish only to illustrate that this person's morbid self-consciousness and his inability to be spontaneous and wholehearted were connected precisely with the lack of consciousness of himself, precisely *the lack of the experience that he was the acting "I."* To be merely an "observer" of one's self, to treat one's self as an object, is to be a stranger to one's self.

The famous centipede is generally a rationalization used by those who do not wish to go through the difficult process of enlarging consciousness of themselves. Furthermore, it is not an accurate fable. The less aware you are of how to drive a car, for example, or of the traffic conditions you are driving through, the more tense you are and the firmer hold you have to keep on yourself. But on the other hand the more experienced you are as a driver and the more conscious you are of the traffic problems and what to do in emergencies, the more you can relax at the wheel with a sense of power. You have the awareness that it is you who are doing the driving, you in control. Consciousness of self actually expands our control of our lives, and with that expanded power comes the capacity to let ourselves go. This is the truth behind the seeming paradox, that the more consciousness of one's self one has, the more spontaneous and creative one can be at the same time.

To be sure, the advice to forget the childish self, the infantile self, is good advice. But it rarely does any good. It is true, furthermore, that one does in one sense forget one's self in creative activity, as we shall see in the next chapter. But first we must consider the difficult question of how one achieves consciousness of himself.

The Experiencing of One's Body and Feelings

In the achieving of consciousness of one's self, most people must start back at the beginning and rediscover their feelings. It is surprising how many people have only a general acquaintance with what they feel—they tell you they feel "fine" or "lousy," as vaguely as though they were saying "China is in the Orient." Their connection with their feelings is as remote as if over a long-distance telephone. They do not feel directly but only give ideas about their feelings; they are not affected by their affects; their emotions give them no motion. Like Eliot's "Hollow Men," they experience themselves as

Shape without form, shade without colour,
Paralyzed force, gesture without motion.

In psychotherapy when such persons are unable to experience their feelings, they often have to learn to feel by answering the question day after day, Just how do I feel right now? What is most important is not how *much* one feels, and we certainly do not mean that it is necessary to effervesce; that is sentimentality rather than sentiment, affectation and not affect. Rather what is important is the experience that it is "I," the active one, who is doing the feeling. This carries with it a directness and immediacy of feeling; one experiences the affect on all levels of one's self. One feels with a heightened aliveness. Then instead of one's feelings being limited like notes in a bugle call, the mature person becomes able to differentiate feelings into as many nuances, strong and passionate experiences, or delicate and sensitive ones, as in the different passages of music in a symphony.

This also means that we need to recover our awareness of our bodies. An infant gets part of his early sense of personal identity through awareness of his body. "We may call the body as experienced by the infant," says Gardner Murphy, "the first core of the self."* The baby reaches his leg time and again, and sooner or later there is the experience, "Here is this leg; I can feel it and it belongs to *me*." Sexual feelings are particularly significant because they are among the earliest feelings which the child can refer directly to himself. When sexual areas are stimulated in play or by clothing, there is the rudimentary beginning of the experience of feeling one's self. Unfortunately sexual feelings and those connected with toilet experiences have been widely tabooed in the past in our society, and the

---

* *Culture and Personality*, eds. Sargent and Smith, p. 19.

child has been given to understand that such feelings are "naughty." Since such feelings are a part of his way of identifying himself, the taboo would clearly imply, "Your image of yourself is dirty." This undoubtedly is one important part of the origin of the tendency to despise the self in our society.

The ability to be aware of one's body has a great importance all through life. It is a curious fact that most adults have so lost physical awareness that they are unable to tell how their leg feels if you should ask them, or their ankle, or their middle finger or any other part of the body. In our society the awareness of the different parts of the body is generally limited to some borderline schizophrenics and other sophisticated people who have come under the influence of yoga or other Eastern exercises. Most people act on the principle, "Let hands or feet feel as they may, I must get off to work." As a result of several centuries of suppressing the body into an inanimate machine, subordinated to the purposes of modern industrialism, people are proud of paying no attention to the body. They treat it as an object for manipulation, as though it were a truck to be driven till it runs out of gas. The only concern they give it is a thought each week as perfunctory as a phone call to a relative to ask how he is, but with really no intention of taking the answer seriously. Nature then comes along, if we may speak metaphorically, and knocks the person down with colds or the flu or more severe illnesses, as though she were saying, "When will you learn to listen to your body?"

The impersonal, separated attitude toward the body is shown also in the way most people, once they become physically ill, react to the sickness. They speak in the passive voice—"I *got* sick," picturing their body as an object just as they would say "I *got* hit by a car." Then they shrug their shoulders and regard their responsibility fulfilled if they go to bed and place themselves completely in the hands of the doctor and the new medical miracle drugs. Thus they use scientific progress as a rationalization for passivity: they know how germs or virus or allergies attack the body, and they also know how penicillin or sulfa or some other drug cures them. The attitude toward disease is not that of the self-aware person who experiences his body as part of himself, but of the compartmentalized person who might express his passive attitude in a sentence like, "The pneumococcus made me sick, but penicillin made me well again."

Certainly it is only common sense to avail one's self of all the help science can give, but that is no reason to surrender one's own sovereignty over one's body. When one does surrender autonomy one opens oneself to psychosomatic ills of all sorts. Many disturbances of bodily function, beginning in such simple things as incorrect walking or faulty posture or breathing, are due to the fact that people have all their lives walked, to take only one simple illustration, as though they were machines, and have never experienced any of the feelings in their feet or legs or rest of the body. The correcting of the malfunction of one's legs, for example, often requires that one learn again to feel what is happening when one walks. In overcoming psychosomatic ills or chronic diseases like tuberculosis, it is essential to learn to "listen to the body" in deciding when to work and when to rest. It is amazing how many hints and guides and intuitions for living come to the sensitive person who has ears to hear what his body is saying. To be tuned to the responses throughout one's body, as well as to be tuned to one's feelings in emotional relations with the world and people around him, is to be on the way to a health which will not break down periodically.

Not only do people separate the body from the self in using it as an instrument for work, but they likewise separate it from the self in their pursuit of pleasure. The body is treated as a vehicle of sensation, from which one can get certain gastronomical pleasures and sexual sensations if skillfully handled, just as though one were tuning a television set. The detached attitude toward sex, which we already noted in a previous chapter, is connected with this tendency to separate the body from the rest of the self. The Kinsey report speaks of the sexual partner as a sexual "object," and in the same vein many persons think in terms of "my sexual *needs* require some outlet," rather than "*I* want and choose sexual relations with this particular person." The tendency to separate sexual activity from the rest of the self is, as everyone knows, illustrated on one hand by the

Puritan attitudes. But it is not so widely realized that libertinism, the opposite to Puritanism, commits exactly the same error of separating sex from the self.

We are proposing welcoming the body back into the union with the self. This means as already suggested recovering an active awareness of one's body. It means *experiencing* one's body—the pleasure of eating or resting or the exhilaration of using toned-up muscles or the gratification of sexual impulses and passion—as aspects of the acting self. It is not the attitude of "My *body* feels" but "*I* feel." In sex it is the attitude of experiencing sexual desire and passion as one aspect of interpersonal relationships. Separating sex from the rest of the self, indeed, is no more tenable than to isolate one's larynx and speak of "my vocal cords wanting to talk with my friend."

We propose, furthermore, placing the self in the center of the picture of bodily health: it is "I" who grow sick or achieve health. We propose the *active* rather than *passive* voice in illness; the old expression "*I sicken*" is accurate. Fortunately in at least one disease the active verb is still used for the process of getting well—tuberculosis patients say "I *cured*" at such-and-such a sanatorium. We propose that illnesses, whether physical or psychological, be taken not as periodic accidents which occur *to* the body (or *to* the "personality" or "mind"), but as nature's means of re-educating the whole person.

Using illness as re-education is illustrated in a letter a patient with tuberculosis wrote to a friend: "The disease occurred not simply because I overworked, or ran athwart some T.B. bugs, but because I was trying to be something I wasn't. I was living as the 'great extrovert,' running here and there, doing three jobs at once, and leaving undeveloped and unused the side of me which would contemplate, would read and think and 'invite my soul' rather than rushing and working at full speed. The disease comes as a demand and an opportunity to rediscover the lost functions of myself. It is as though the disease were nature's way of saying, 'You must become your whole self. To the extent that you do not, you will be ill; and you will become well only to the extent that you do become yourself.'" We may add that it is an actual clinical fact that some persons, viewing their illnesses as an opportunity for re-education, become more healthy both psychologically and physically, more fulfilled as persons, after a serious illness than before.

This way of experiencing illness and health will help us overcome the dichotomy between body and mind which has so bedeviled modern man. When one looks at the different illnesses from the perspective of the self, he sees that physical, psychological and spiritual (using the last term to refer to despair and the sense of meaninglessness in life) diseases are all aspects of the same difficulty of the self in finding itself in its world. It is well known, for example, that the different kinds of illness may serve interchangeable purposes for the individual. Physical illness may relieve psychological troubles by giving some focus for "floating" anxiety—the person then has something concrete to worry about, and that is a lot less painful than vague "floating" anxiety; or by giving needed respite from responsibility to those who have not learned to assume responsibility maturely. And many a person, through a bout of influenza or more serious disease, has "relieved" his guilt feelings, however unconstructive such a method may be. Thus so long as scientific progress takes away diphtheria, tuberculosis and other diseases—a consummation devoutly to be wished—*without* helping people to get over their anxiety, guilt, emptiness and purposelessness, sickness is only forced into a new channel. That may sound like a rash statement, but in principle I believe it is true. The struggle against disease in the compartmentalized way is like Hercules' battle against the seven-headed Hydra—every time he cut off one head, another grew in its place. The battle for health must be won on the deeper level of the integration of the self. Certainly it is no depreciation of the great value of the new medical discoveries to emphasize that we shall make lasting progress in health only to the extent that we go beyond finding means of killing germs and bacilli and external organisms which invade the body, and discover means of helping ourselves and other people so to affirm their own beings that they will not need to be sick.

Awareness of one's feelings lays the groundwork for the second step: knowing what one *wants*. This point may look very simple at first glance—who does not know what he wants? But as we pointed out in the first chapter, the amazing thing is how few people actually do. If one looks honestly into himself, does he not find that most of what he thinks he wants is just routine—like fish on Friday; or that what he wants is what he thinks he *should* want—like being a success in his work; or *wants* to want—like loving his neighbor? One can often see clearly the expression of direct and honest wants in children before they have been taught to falsify their desires. The child exclaims, "I *like* ice cream, I *want* a cone," and there is no confusion about who wants what. Such directness of desire often comes like a breath of fresh air in a murky land. It may not be best that he have the cone at the time, and it is obviously the parents' responsibility to say Yes or No if the child is not mature enough to decide. But let the parents not teach the child to falsify his emotions by trying to persuade him that he does not want the cone!

To be aware of one's feelings and desires does not at all imply expressing them indiscriminately wherever one happens to be. Judgment and decision, as we shall see later, are part of any mature consciousness of self. But how is one going to have a basis for judging what he will or will not do unless he first knows what he *wants*? For an adolescent to be aware that he has erotic impulses toward some person of the opposite sex sitting across from him in the streetcar, or towards his mother, does not at all mean that he acts on these impulses. But suppose he never lets these impulses reach the threshold of awareness because they are not socially acceptable? How is he then to know years later, when he is married, whether he engages in sexual relations with his wife because he really wants to, or whether because this is then the acceptable and "expected" act, the routine thing to do?

People who voice with alarm the caution that unless desires and emotions are suppressed they will pop out every which way, and everyone, for example, will be overcome by sexual desire for his mother or his best friend's wife, are talking about *neurotic* emotions. As a matter of fact, we know that it is precisely the emotions and desires which have been repressed which later return to drive the person compulsively. The Victorian gyroscope kind of man had to control his emotions rigidly, for, by virtue of having locked them up in jail, he had turned them into lawbreakers. But the more integrated a person is, the less compulsive become his emotions. In the mature person feelings and wants occur in a *configuration.* In seeing a dinner as part of a drama on the stage, to give a simple example, one is not consumed with desire for food; one came to see a drama and not to eat. Or when listening to a concert singer, one is not consumed with sexual desire even though she may be very attractive; the configuration is set by the fact that one chose in coming to hear music. Of course, as we have indicated throughout this book, none of us escape conflicts from time to time. But these are different from being compulsively driven by emotions.

Every direct and immediate experience of feeling and wanting is spontaneous and unique. That is to say, the wanting and feeling are uniquely part of that particular situation at that particular time and place. Spontaneity means to be able to respond directly to the total picture—or, as it is technically called, to respond to the "figure-ground configuration." Spontaneity is the active "I" becoming part of the figure-ground. In a good portrait painting the background is always an integral part of the portrait; so an act of a mature human being is an integral part of the self in relation to the world around it. Spontaneity, thus, is very different from effervescence or egocentricity, or letting out one's feelings regardless of the environment. Spontaneity, rather, is the acting "I" responding to a particular environment at a given moment. The originality and uniqueness which is always part of a spontaneous feeling can be understood in this light. For just as there never was exactly that situation before and never will be again, so the feeling one has at that time is new and never to be exactly repeated. It is only neurotic behavior which is rigidly repetitive.

The third step, along with rediscovering our feelings and wants, is to recover our relation with the subconscious aspects of ourselves. We shall add only some brief comments about this step. As modern man has given up sovereignty over his body, so also he has surrendered the unconscious side of his personality, and it has become almost alien to him. In earlier chapters we have seen how the suppression of the "irrational," subjective and unconscious aspects of experience went hand in hand with modern man's need to emphasize regular, rational work in the world of industry and commerce. Now we need to find and welcome back, so far as we can, what we suppressed. All through the ages, even before the time when Joseph interpreted the dreams of Pharaoh until the modern period, people have regarded their dreams, for example, as sources of wisdom, guidance and insight. But most of us today think of our dreams as odd episodes, as foreign as some strange ceremonial dance in Tibet. This results in the cutting off of an exceedingly great and significant portion of the self. We are then no longer able to use much of the wisdom and power of the unconscious. It puts us in the position of trying to drive a chariot with reins attached to only one horse, in Plato's time-honored figure, with the four or five other horses pulling off in different directions. Though the tendencies and intuitions in the unconscious are blocked off from our conscious awareness, they are still part of the self and accessible in various degrees to being made conscious. The sooner we recover sovereignty in that portion of the kingdom the better.

To go into dream interpretation in any detail would take us too far afield from our topic in this chapter. Understanding dreams is of course a subtle and complex matter—though it is not so complex as one would think when he reads about the esoteric symbols in much modern dream interpretation. These esoteric symbols put the whole problem back into a foreign language again—and that is another way, perhaps the typically modern way, of surrendering our sovereignty over the unconscious aspects of ourselves. As though we were saying, the authorities and those who know the magic answers can understand our dreams, but we cannot ourselves! Dr. Erich Fromm's recent book, *The Forgotten Language*, points out that dreams, like myths and fairy tales, are not at all a foreign language, but are in reality part of the one universal language shared by all mankind. Fromm's book is to be recommended to the nontechnical reader who wishes to relearn something about this subconscious "language of his fatherland."

In this chapter we wish only to bespeak a sympathetic attitude toward dreams and other expressions of the subconscious and unconscious aspects of ourselves. Dreams are expressions not only of conflicts and repressed desires, but also of previous knowledge that one has learned, possibly many years before, and thinks he has forgotten. Even the unskilled person, if he takes the attitude that what his dreams tell him is not simply to be rejected as silly, may get occasional useful guidance from his dreams. And the person who has become skillful in the understanding of what he is saying to himself in his dreams can get from them, from time to time, marvelously valuable hints and insights into solutions to his problems.

THE UPSHOT of this chapter has been to show that the more self-awareness a person has, the more alive he is. "The more consciousness," remarked Kierkegaard, "the more self." Becoming a person means this heightened awareness, this heightened experience of "I-ness," this experience that it is I, the acting one, who is the subject of what is occurring.

This view of what it means to become a person, in conclusion, saves us from two errors. The first is *passivism**—letting the deterministic forces in one's experience take the place of self-awareness. It must be admitted that some tendencies in the older forms of psychoanalysis can be used to rationalize passivism. It was the epoch-making discovery of Freud to show how much every person is "pushed" by unconscious fears, desires and tendencies of all sorts, and that man is really much less a master in the household of his own mind than the nineteenth-century man of "will power" fondly believed. But a harmful implication was carried along with this emphasis on the determinism of unconscious forces, which Freud himself partly succumbed to. The early psychotherapist Grodeck, for example, wrote, "We are

---

* I use this word for the unconstructive (neurotic) form of passivity. Some forms of passivity, such as reverie and relaxation, may be normal and constructive: but in those forms, the self is still in the center of awareness; it is "I" who am relaxing or in reverie.

lived by our unconscious," and Freud in a letter commended him for his emphasis on the "passivity of the ego." But we must underline, to correct a partial misunderstanding, that the over-all purpose of Freud's exploration of the unconscious forces was to help people bring these forces into consciousness. The goal of psychoanalysis, as he said time and again, was to make the unconscious conscious; to enlarge the scope of awareness; to help the individual become aware of the unconscious tendencies which have tended to push the self around like mutinous sailors who have seized power below the deck of the ship; and thus to help the person consciously direct his own ship. Hence the emphasis in this chapter on the heightened awareness of one's self, and the warning against passivism, have much in common with the over-all purpose of Freud's thought.

The other error this view of the person enables us to avoid is *activism*—that is, using *activity* as a substitute for *awareness*. By activism we mean the tendency, so common in this country, to assume that the more one is acting, the more one is alive. It should be clear that when we have used the term "the active I" in this book, we have not meant busyness or merely doing things. Many people keep busy all the time as a way of covering up anxiety; their activism is a way of running from themselves. They get a pseudo and temporary sense of aliveness by being in a hurry, as though something is going on if they are but moving, and as though being busy is a proof of one's importance. Chaucer has a sly and astute comment about this type, represented in the merchant in *Canterbury Tales*, "Methinks he seemed busier than he was."

Our emphasis on self-awareness certainly includes acting as an expression of the alive, integrated self, but it is the opposite to activism— the opposite, that is, to acting as an escape from self-awareness. Aliveness often means the capacity not to act, to be creatively idle—which may be more difficult for most modern people than to do something. "To be idle," Robert Louis Stevenson accurately wrote, "requires a strong sense of personal identity." Self-awareness, as we have proposed it, brings back into the picture the quieter kinds of aliveness— the arts of contemplation and meditation for example, which the

4

The Struggle to Be

❧

BUT is not the path to self-awareness fraught with more vicissitudes, more peaks and precipices of difficulty and conflict than implied in the foregoing chapter? True; and we now turn to the more dynamic aspects of becoming a person. For most people, particularly adults trying to overcome the earlier experiences which have blocked them in becoming persons in their own right, achieving consciousness of self involves struggle and conflict. They find that becoming persons requires not only learning to feel, to experience and to want, as we pointed out in the preceding chapter, but to fight against what prevents them from feeling and wanting. They discover that there are certain chains which hold them back. These chains, in essence, are the ties which bind them to the parents, especially in our society to the mother.

We have seen that the human being's development is a continuum of differentiation from the "mass" toward freedom as an individual. We have also noted that the potential person is originally a unity with the mother as a foetus in the womb, where it is fed automatically through the umbilical cord without any choice by mother or baby. When it is born and the physical umbilical cord is cut, it has become a physical individual, and feeding thereafter involves some conscious choice on the part of both parties—the infant can raise a howl in demand for food, and the mother can say Yes or No. But the infant still is almost completely dependent on the parents, particularly the mother, who nurses him. His becoming an individual continues through an infinite number of steps—the emergence of consciousness of self with the rudimentary beginnings of responsibility and freedom, the movement out from the parental yard when he goes to school, the maturation into a sexual individual at puberty, the struggles of going out on his own to college and in making vocational choices, the assuming of responsibility for a new family in marriage, and so on. All through life a person is engaged in this continuum of differentiation of himself from the whole, followed by steps toward new integration. Indeed, all evolution can be described as the process of differentiation of the part from the whole, the individual from the mass, with the parts then relating to each other on a higher level. Since the human being, in contrast to a stone or chemical compound, can fulfill his individuality only by conscious and responsible choice, he must become a psychological and ethical as well as a physical individual.

Strictly speaking, the process of being born from the womb, cutting free from the mass, replacing dependency with choice, is involved in every decision of one's life, and even is the issue facing one on his deathbed. For what is the capacity to die courageously except the ultimate step in the continuum of learning to be on one's own, to leave the whole?

Thus every person's life could be portrayed by a graph of differentiation—how far has he freed himself from automatic dependencies, become an individual, able then to relate to his fellows on the new level of self-chosen love, responsibility and creative work? We now turn to the psychological struggles involved in this differentiation of the person from the mass.

Cutting the Psychological Umbilical Cord

The baby becomes a physical individual when the umbilical cord is severed at his birth, but unless the psychological umbilical cord is also in due time cut, he remains like a toddler tied to a stake in his parents' front yard. He can go no farther than the length of his rope. His development is blocked, and the surrendered freedom for growth turns inward and festers in resentment and anger. These are the people who, though they may seem to get along tolerably well within the range of the toddler's rope, are greatly upset when they confront marriage, or when they go off to work or eventually face death. In every crisis they tend figuratively or literally to go "back to mother." As one young husband put it, "I cannot love my wife enough because I love my mother too much." His only error was in using the word "love" for his relation to his mother. Real love is expansive and never excludes loving others: it is only being *tied* to the mother which is exclusive and blocks one's loving one's wife. In our time the tendency to remain enchained is particularly strong, since when a society is so disrupted that it is no longer a "mother" in the sense of giving the individual minimal consistent support, he tends to cling much more closely to the physical mother of his childhood.

An actual case may help us see more concretely what these ties are like, and the difficulties involved in cutting them. The following case is not extraordinary; indeed, almost the only unusual aspect of it is that the mother's behavior was not so subtle or disguised as in many cases. A gifted man of thirty was troubled with homosexual feelings, lack of any positive feelings towards women but very great fears of them at the same time. He avoided intimacy with anyone, and also he was blocked in his completion of his doctoral dissertation for his graduate degree. An only child, he had developed a contempt for his father, who was weak and under the mother's domination. The mother had often belittled the father in the boy's presence; he once overheard her saying to the father in an argument, "You are worth more to us dead than alive, but you have always been a coward and you are afraid to take your own life." The boy had been dressed carefully by his mother when he went to school, was not able to fight, and his mother would come to school when necessary to protect him from the rougher boys. She would intimately confide in the boy at length, telling him how much she suffered with the father, and required him to help her with some toilet functions, a practice he greatly disliked. Even in college days when he returned for vacation he would be paralyzed with anxiety when hearing his mother coming up the stairs at night for fear she would come into his room when he was undressed. She had carried on an extramarital affair rather openly when he was a boy, which upset him greatly, and, as often happens in such situations, it made him much more jealous of her attentions. Later on in adolescence she tried to block his meeting girls but when he dated anyway, she endeavored to make dates for him with girls whose families could enhance her social position.

When he was a boy, much was made of his piano playing and recitations in school and Sunday school. One time he greatly embarrassed his parents at Sunday-school exercises by being unable to recite the commandment "Honor thy mother and father"; and when his mother would have him play the piano at ladies' meetings, he would forget the piece no matter how well he had known it beforehand. He was a very bright boy and had many successes in school and later gained some prestige in the armed forces, but these were treated by his mother as ways of enhancing her own prestige in the community. The reader has no doubt already noticed that his blockage in completing his doctoral work had much in common with his forgetting the piano solo; both were rebellions against his mother's exploitation of his successes. For one way to defend yourself against someone's exploiting your successes is to accomplish nothing which the other could take away. The mother's frequent letters to him at the time of his therapy were long complaints and descriptions of her minor heart attacks, together with outright requests that he come home and take responsibility for her and hints that she would have another attack if he didn't show more interest.

The problems of this young man, which we have described in a somewhat oversimplified way, are in several ways typical of many young men in our society. First, he suffered from lack of feeling, confusion of sexual role and a lack of potency—both sexually and in his work. A second relatively typical aspect is the family pattern. It will be noted that this family is significantly different from the patriarchal families which Freud had in mind when he first formulated his oedipus doctrine. In our young man's family the mother was the dominating figure, the father was weak and pictured as somewhat contemptible to the son. The third aspect is that the boy had been favored by the mother, made prince consort and placed in the father's position, this preferential treatment to continue so long as the boy pleased the mother. But "Uneasy lies the head that wears a crown." The young man derived no real sense of security and power from his position on the throne, for he was there not because of his own strength but as a puppet of the mother. The classical oedipus picture is present in this case, to be sure, but with important differences: the boy is deathly afraid of castration (losing his power), but it is the mother who castrates him, not the father. The father is not much of a rival—the mother has seen to that. The son has had no figure of masculine strength to identify with, so he lacks that normal source of the experience of power for a growing boy. As a substitute for this lack of power he has only his mother's adulation, pampering and domineering attention. As would be expected, such a young man had frequent dreams of being literally a prince. His narcissism was very great, for it had to compensate for his actual, inner feeling that he was almost completely powerless. He could rebel a little against his mother by *not* accomplishing things and by occasional verbal spats, but this was only the passive protest of a slave toward its master. It is not in the slightest surprising that this man should be deathly afraid of women; nor is it surprising that he should be in so much inward conflict that he would be unable to move ahead in work, love, or any intimacy with persons.

What is the way out of such a morbid intertwining? Of course a child can temporarily withdraw, seeking to protect himself from exploitation by making himself as little as possible, and thus try to "avoid the slings and arrows of outrageous fortune." One young man, looking back on a boyhood in which he was caught in the cross fire between a weak, alcoholic father and a dominating, martyr-type mother, described in a poem how he saw himself in those early years,

You stand there by the table,
Still clutching your teddy bear. . . .

Make it so small they'll fail
To find it. . . .
Then you're left
Alone
To defend what they didn't want—
Not being able to find it.

Or—and this generally occurs later—he can try to "take arms against a sea of troubles," and struggle actively to achieve his freedom as a person in his own right. To this we now turn.

The Struggle against Mother

The struggle for such freedom is presented in one of the greatest dramas of all times, that of Orestes. Let us look at the problem through the insights of that drama. This will help not only because a historical perspective gives us new light on the present, but also because the profoundest truths of human experience, like those in the drama of Oedipus or the Book of Job, can be seen most clearly in the classical forms which have endured age after age.

This great story of human conflict was written first by Aeschylus in ancient Greece, and recently has been retold in modern verse by Robinson Jeffers in "The Tower Beyond Tragedy." While Agamemnon, King of Mycenae, is off leading the Greek armies in the war against Troy, his wife Clytemnestra takes her uncle Aegisthus as her lover. When Agamemnon returns from Troy, she murders him. She then exiles her infant son Orestes from the kingdom and keeps her daughter Electra in a servile position. When Orestes comes of age, he returns to Mycenae to kill his mother. Facing him with his drawn sword in front of the palace, Clytemnestra tries to get his pity by blaming his father, "Hard was my lot, my child"; and then she resorts to threats, crying, "My curse beware, the mother's curse that bore thee!" And when these strategies do not work, as Robinson Jeffers pictures it, she finally tries to seduce Orestes with false protestations of her love, embracing him and kissing him passionately. He suddenly goes limp, drops his sword with the words, "I will be passive, I am blunted." The amazing thing about this sudden, inert passivity is that it is so vividly what every psychotherapist today observes in the cases of many young men, an acting out of the loss of potency in their struggle with a dominating mother. It is only when Orestes notes that the mother quickly takes advantage of his moment of passivity to summon her soldiers, and realizes that her so-called love is not love at all but a strategy for getting him under her power, that he arises, regains his strength, and strikes the blow.

Then Orestes in effect goes mad. He is pursued by the "Furies," the punishing "spirits of the night" with their locks "entwined with knotted snakes." These are the Greek mythological figures impersonating self-reproach and a bad conscience, and again it is astonishing how keenly and accurately the ancient Greeks describe these symbols of the gnawing guilt which will not let a person sleep, and may push him into neurosis or even psychosis.

Orestes is driven, sleepless and weary, by the Furies until finally he falls with his arms around Apollo's altar at Delphi, where temporarily he receives a respite. Then, under Apollo's protection, he is sent to Athens where he is tried before a large court presided over by Athena. The tremendous issue to be decided is whether a person is to be judged guilty for killing a dominating and exploitative parent. Since the outcome will in actuality be crucial for the future of mankind, the gods from Olympus come down to participate in the debate. After many speeches, Athena makes the charge to the jury, in which she adjures them not to "cast from your walls all high authority," to preserve "reverence of the gods and holy fear," and to avoid the twin perils of "anarchy" on one hand and "slavish masterdom" on the other. The jury votes; and it is a tie. So Athena herself, the goddess of civic virtues, objectivity and wisdom, has to cast the deciding vote. She announces to the court that if mankind is to advance persons must become free from the chains to such hating parents, even though it involves killing the parent. And so by her vote Orestes is forgiven.

Underneath this bare outline lies a terrifying struggle of human passions, a conflict as profound and basic as any in human experience. The theme is the killing of the mother but the meaning really is the struggle of Orestes, the son, for his existence as a person. It is nothing less than the struggle "to be or not to be" a psychological and spiritual being. As Athena and others make clear in the speeches at the trial, it is a debate between the "old" ways, customs and morals, represented by the spirit of Clytemnestra and the Erinyes, the sisters from the dark underground, and the "new," advocated by Apollo and Athena and personified by Orestes' act. The stories can, of course, be interpreted sociologically as the struggle of the new patriarchy against the old matriarchy, as Erich Fromm does in his book *The Forgotten Language*. We are concerned here, however, with the psychological implications of the conflict.

With a fascinating psychological acumen, Aeschylus points out that "Orestes could not choose but scale the height," and that he would have been "sick" forever if he had not done the deed. And in the concluding crescendo Aeschylus has the Greek chorus sing, "The Light has come, the day dawns clear." That is to say, with Orestes' deed new light and clarification come into the world.

To many people the most shocking thing about this drama, when we relate it to problems of today, will be not what it says about Orestes, but in its implication that some mothers are like Clytemnestra. To be sure, Clytemnestra is an extreme figure; no human being's motives are really unmixed hate or love or desire for power, but rather are complex blendings of these motives. It is true that Clytemnestra is a symbol more than a person—a symbol for the dominating and authoritarian tendencies in the parent which would "exile" and strangle the potentialities of the child. And it is true also that this drama, with the usual profoundness and courage of the Greek literature, minces no words in presenting these basic human conflicts. Most of us in the modern day, fed a more superficial diet, find this medicine too strong for our taste.

What does the killing of the parent mean? The essence of the struggle is that the growing person, in this case Orestes, fights against the authoritarian powers which would strangle his growth and freedom.

Such powers in the family circle may head up more in the father or in the mother. Freud, indeed, believed it more or less universally true that the conflict would be between father and son—that the father would try to exile, to take away the power of, to "castrate" the son; and that the son, like Oedipus, would have to kill his father to gain his own right to exist. We now know, however, that the oedipus "complex" is not universal, but depends on cultural and historical factors. Freud grew up in the society of the "German father." There is much evidence in our middle of the twentieth century in this country that the mother, not the father, has been the dominant figure in the families of persons who are now, let us say, between twenty and fifty, that the relation to her presents the greatest problem, and that the Orestes myth is the one which they feel expresses most profoundly their own experience. I speak not only on the basis of the deeper feelings and dreams of people with whom I have worked professionally in psychotherapy, but also out of the experience of other therapists with whom I have talked. As in the case we described earlier, the son is often enchained to the mother in the respect that he learns to get his rewards only by pleasing her. It is as though the son's potency is accessible to him only for the purpose of living up to the high expectations of his mother. And of course potency is not power at all when it is available only at someone else's command. Thus obviously he is not able to use his power for the development of himself as a person or in loving other people until he becomes free from his ties to her.

As we describe the conflict with dominating mothers, some readers may be reminded of the arguments about "Momism" which have recently been current.

How much truth there is in the charges of "Momism" I don't pretend to know. My guess, however, is that a good deal of the "generation of vipers" type of writing is a way of getting out vituperation against the mother when the real thing underneath that makes one so angry is one's own dependence on her. However that may be, there is still plenty of evidence that the system "in our country is beginning to resemble a matriarchy," as the psychiatrist Edward A. Strecker points out. The psychoanalyst Erik Erikson, discussing in *Childhood and Society* the origins of this matriarchal development, feels that "Mom is more the victim than the victor," and that the American mother was forced into the position of power because the father—at work in the city five days a week and around the house only on week ends—abdicated the central position in the family. "Mother became 'Mom' only when Father became 'Pop'."

Matriarchy is one thing, but we still have the question of why there is such a *demanding* quality in the power the women exert in our latter-day matriarchy. We should emphasize, by the way, that we are not talking about the *present* generation of mothers; they are in general confused. It is particularly out of the previous generation of mothers that these problems arose in our society. I do not know the psychosociological causes of the situation. All we can do is note that the mothers of these patients in psychotherapy, like the castrating mother of the young man in the case cited above, behave as though they had suffered some great disappointment. Clytemnestra said that she did what she did "from an age old hate." Certainly no one like Clytemnestra endeavors to exercise such exploitative and demanding power unless there is good reason for it; generally the reason is that she has been greatly hurt herself, and feels that the only way to protect herself from future suffering is to dominate others. Is it that women of that previous generation in our society were given some tremendous expectations of what they would receive from men? Was it a result of the frontier psychology in which women had a special value, merging with attitudes of the late Victorian period when women were placed on a pedestal? Were these women then given the expectation that they would be forever served? And in the process was their function as women radically frustrated in some way? Actually we know that this late Victorian generation of women was a very frustrated group sexually, and very possibly in other ways as well. For how could women simply enjoy and have gratification being women when they were worshiped on pedestals on the frontier and expected to civilize the frontier at the same time? Is the answer to our question that this generation of mothers, having been led to expect wonderful things from men, were deeply disappointed in their husbands, and take out this disappointment in excessive possessiveness and domination of the son?

Probably all of these points have something to do with the mother-child tie in our particular society. But the Greeks, not content to present these questions sociologically and psychologically, proceed to shake the foundations of our discussion by suggesting, naively enough, that there may be some biological tie between mother and child which makes the child's becoming free from the mother so crucial and difficult. This question is raised in the drama in the fact that the goddess who casts the vote which forgives Orestes is Athena—the goddess who, as she puts it, "never knew the mother's womb that bore me," but sprang, full-attired, from the forehead of her father, Zeus.

This is a startling idea to meditate on. The birth without benefit of womb is amazing enough to begin with, but it becomes even staggering when we consider the implications of the fact that the Greeks made this Athena the goddess of *wisdom*. She says she votes for Orestes because she, never having existed in the womb, is on the side of the "new." Does this imply that the human being's pilgrimage from dependence, prejudice and immaturity toward independence, wisdom and maturity is so difficult at best, so hobbled by ties to physical and psychological umbilical cords, that the mythological goddess of wisdom and civic virtue must be pictured as one who never had to fight against the umbilical cord? We know that the infant is closer to the mother, in whose womb he gestates and from whose breast he is fed, than to the father: are the Greeks implying that since the child is blood of the mother's blood and flesh of her flesh, he will always be bound by his tie to her, and that the mother relationship will always tend to be *conserving* rather than *revolutionary*, oriented to the past more than to the future? The Greeks knew better than to imply that wisdom exists in a vacuum of unrelatedness; or that there is anything wrong in ties as such. But they may mean that the temptation to be "sheltered," to regress, to be "passive" and "blunted" as Orestes puts it, are symbolized by the tendency to go back into the womb, and that maturity and freedom as an individual are the opposite to these tendencies. Is this the reason their goddess of wisdom "never knew the womb"?

We shall leave these questions for the reader to answer as he sees fit, and return to Orestes. For our real interest here is in how this young man, as the prototype of the person in emotional conflict, achieves his freedom to live as a person. In his temporary madness after performing the deed, Orestes wanders through the forest "sick with visions." Robinson Jeffers in his version pictures Orestes then coming back to the palace at Mycenae, where his sister Electra invites him to become king in his father's place. Orestes looks at her in amazement and asks how she can be so unperceptive as to think that he went through the terrible deed of killing his mother just to be king of Mycenae in Agamemnon's place. No, he has "outgrown the city," and has resolved to leave. Electra, assuming that his trouble is that he "needs a woman," proposes to marry him. He then exclaims, "It is Clytemnestra in you," and he points out that the whole trouble in their unfortunate family has been incest. In his struggles in the forest, he continues,

> . . . I saw a vision of us move in the dark; all that we did or
>   dreamed of
> Regarded each other, the man pursued the woman, the woman
>   clung to the man, warriors and kings
> Strained at each other in the darkness, all loved or fought
>   inward, each one of the lost people
> Sought the eyes of another that another should praise him;
>   sought never his own but another's. . . .
> . . . when they look backward they see only a man standing at
>   the beginning,
> Or forward, a man at the end; or if upward, men in the shining
>   bitter sky striding and feasting,
> Whom you call Gods. . . .
> It is all turned inward, all your desires incestuous. . . .*

---

* Robinson Jeffers, "The Tower Beyond Tragedy," from *Roan Stallion*. Reprinted by permission of Random House, Inc. Copyright 1925 by Boni & Liveright.

For himself, Orestes has resolved that he "will not waste inward." If he should accede to her pleading and remain in Mycenae, he tells his sister, he would be "like a stone walking"—that is to say, he would have forfeited his unique nature as a human being and would have become inorganic. As he walks out, "toward humanity" and away from the incestuous nest of Mycenae, he concludes with a phrase which could ring down the corridors of centuries as the goal of man's psychological integration, *I have fallen in love outward.*

It is by no accident that Orestes uses the terms "inward" and "outward" several times in these few lines, and that he says the main trouble in Mycenae has been "incest." For incest is simply the sexual, physical symbol of being turned inward on the family, and of being unable, correspondingly, to "love outwardly." Psychologically, incestuous desires, when they continue past adolescence, are the sexual symptom of morbid dependency on the parent, and they occur predominantly in persons who have not "grown up," have not cut the psychological umbilical cord which binds them to the parent. Sexual gratification is then not too different from the oral gratification the child receives in being fed by the mother. Prominent, also, in incestuous relations is, as Orestes says, the need to be admired by the other, "that another should praise him."

With the special acumen of poetry, Jeffers has Orestes say that even the religion of these people is incestuous. They see only projections of themselves in the sky, "men striding and feasting" whom they call gods. Their gods are expressions not of new and higher levels of aspiration and integration, but of their own need to turn back to infantile dependencies. Religiously and psychologically this is, of course, the exact opposite to what Jesus proclaims, "I have come not to bring peace but a sword. For I am come to set a man at variance against his father, and the daughter against her mother, and the daughter-in-law against her mother-in-law. And a man's foes shall be they of his own household."* Obviously Jesus is not preaching hatred and division as such, but he means to state in the most radical form

---

* Matthew 10:34–36.

that spiritual development is *away* from incest and *toward* the capacity to love the neighbor and stranger. The members of "a man's own household will be his foes" in truth if he is still bound to them.

The taboo against incest found in almost every society has sound psycho-social merit in that it makes for the introduction of "new blood" and "new genes," or, more accurately, the enlarging of the possibilities of change and development. Incest does not do physical harm to the baby: it merely doubles the same heredity in the child, and robs it of the possibilities it would have if the parent had married outside the family. That is to say, the prohibition against incest makes for greater differentiation in human development, and requires that integration be found not through sameness, but on a higher level. Thus we can add to our statement at the beginning of this chapter, that *the continuum of differentiation which is the life pilgrimage of the human being requires developing away from incest and toward the capacity to "love outwardly."*

The Struggle against One's Own Dependency

Obviously, the moral of the Orestes drama is not that everyone get a gun and kill his mother. What has to be killed, as we have already implied, is the infantile ties of dependency which binds the person to the parents, and thereby keeps him from loving outwardly and creating independently.

This is no simple job to be initiated by a sudden resolution and performed in one great burst of freedom, nor is it accomplished by one big "blow-up" against one's parents. The Orestes drama, as dramas do, condenses the "struggle to be" into a few weeks. Actually in real life it is a matter of long, uphill growth to new levels of integration— growth meaning not automatic process but re-education, finding new insights, making self-conscious decisions, and throughout being willing to face occasional or frequent bitter struggles. A person in psychotherapy often must work through his patterns for months to discover how much he has been tied without knowing it, and to see time and again that this enchainment underlies his inability to love, to work, or to marry. He then finds that the struggle to become a person in his own right often brings considerable anxiety and occasionally some actual terror. It is not surprising that those who are fighting to break such chains go through terrific emotional upsets and conflicts, comparable to Orestes' temporary madness. The conflict is in essence that of moving out from a protected, familiar place into new independence, from support to temporary isolation, while at the same time one feels one's own anxiety and powerlessness. The struggle takes a severe (that is, neurotic) form when the individual has been unable to grow at previous stages in his development; thus neurotic conflicts have grown, and the eventual break is more traumatic and radical. The conflict between Orestes and his mother had to occur in that traumatic way because of the previous hatreds, incestuous relations and morbidity in the interpersonal relations in Mycenae.

What keeps the person tied to the parent? Aeschylus, typically Greek, portrays the source of the problem as *objective*—certain evil things have gone on for several generations in the royal family at Mycenae, and Orestes therefore could do nothing except choose to kill his mother. Shakespeare, typically modern, presents Hamlet's similar "struggle to be" as an internal, subjective conflict with his own conscience, guilt, ambivalent courage and indecisiveness. The truth is that Aeschylus and Shakespeare are both right: such struggles are both inward and outward. The authoritarian shackling which the person endures earliest in life is external: the growing infant, whether a child of exploitative parents or, let us say, a Jew born in a country with anti-Semitic prejudice, is the victim of the external circumstances. The child must face and adjust to, by hook or crook, the world he is born into. But gradually in anyone's development the authoritarian problem becomes *internalized:* the growing person takes over the rules and plants them in himself; and he tends to act all his life as though he still were fighting the original forces which would enslave him. But it now has become an *internal* conflict. Fortunately, there is a happy moral in this point: since the person has taken over the suppressive forces and keeps them going in himself, he also has in himself the power to get over them.

For adults, then, who are engaged in rediscovering themselves, the battle is centrally an internal one. *The struggle to become a person takes place within the person himself.* None of us can avoid taking a stand against exploitative persons or external forces in the environment, to be sure, but the crucial psychological battle we must wage is that against our own dependent needs, and our anxiety and guilt feelings which will arise as we move toward freedom. The basic conflict, in fine, is between that part of the person which seeks growth, expansion and health against the part which longs to remain on an immature level, tied still to the psychological umbilical cord and receiving the pseudo-protection and pampering of the parent in exchange for independence.

Stages in Consciousness of Self

We have seen that becoming a person means going through several stages of consciousness of one's self. The first is that of the *innocence* of the infant before consciousness of self is born. The second is the stage of *rebellion*, when the person is trying to become free to establish some inner strength in his own right. This stage is most clearly seen in the child of two or three or the adolescent, and may involve defiance and hostility, as shown in extreme form in Orestes' fight for his freedom. In greater or lesser degree rebellion is a necessary transition as one cuts old ties and seeks to make new ones. But rebellion is not to be confused with freedom.

The third stage we may call *the ordinary consciousness of self.* In this stage a person can to some extent see his errors, make some allowance for his prejudices, use his guilt feelings and anxiety as experiences to learn from, and make his decisions with some responsibility. This is what most people mean when they speak of a healthy state of personality.

But there is a fourth stage of consciousness which is extraordinary in the sense that most individuals experience it only rarely. This stage is most clearly illustrated when one gets a sudden insight into a problem—abruptly, seemingly from nowhere, pops up an answer for which one has struggled in vain for days. Sometimes such insights come in dreams, or at moments of reverie when one is thinking about something else: in any case, we know that the answer emerges from what are called subconscious levels in the personality. Such consciousness may occur in scientific, religious or artistic activity alike; it is sometimes popularly called "dawning" of ideas or "inspiration." As all students of creative activity make clear, this level of consciousness is present in all creative work.

What shall this level be called? "Objective self-consciousness," as it would be termed in some Oriental thinking, because of the glimpses it affords into objective truth? Or "self-surpassing consciousness," as Nietzsche might call it? Or "self-transcending consciousness," in the ethical-religious tradition? All these terms distort as well as clarify. I propose a term which is less dramatic but perhaps, for our day, more satisfactory, *creative consciousness of self.*

The classical psychological term for this awareness is *ecstasy.* The word literally means "to stand outside one's self," that is, to catch a view of, or experience something, from a perspective outside one's usual limited viewpoint. Ordinarily what a person sees in the *objective* world around him is always more or less distorted and clouded by the fact that he sees it *subjectively.* As human beings, what we see is always through personal eyes, and interpreted by each person through his own private world; we are always dogged, that is, by a dichotomy between subjectivity and objectivity. This fourth level of consciousness cuts below the split between objectivity and subjectivity. Temporarily we can transcend the usual limits of conscious personality. Through what is called insight, or intuition, or the other only vaguely understood processes which are involved in creativity, we may get glimpses of objective truth as it exists in reality, or sense some new ethical possibility in, let us say, an experience of unselfish love.

This is what Orestes experienced in his thoughts while wandering in the forest after the deed.

> . . . they have not made words for it, to go behind things, beyond
>   hours and ages,
> And be all things in all time . . .

   . . . how can I express the excellence I have found, that has no
     color but clearness;
No honey but ecstasy . . .
   . . . no desire but fulfilled, no passion but peace . . .*

Lest the point be obscured for some readers by Jeffers' poetic language, let us emphasize that what Orestes means can be described
fairly well in psychological terms. It is simply a further stage of the
fact that he has been able to overcome the tendency of the men in
Mycenae to see only themselves in other people's eyes, "all turned
inward," all preoccupied with the projections of their own prejudices,
which they in their conceit name "truth." To be, rather, "turned outward" means to pierce in imagination beyond what one knows at the
moment. It is not unscientific sentimentality to point out, as Nietzsche and almost every other writer on ethics has done, that man in
fulfilling himself goes through a process of "transcending" himself.
This is simply one side of the basic characteristics of the growing,
healthy human being, that from moment to moment he is enlarging
his awareness of himself and his world. "Life is occupied in both per-
petuating itself and in surpassing itself," Simone de Beauvoir points
out in her book on ethics; "if all it does is maintain itself, then living
is only not dying, and human existence is indistinguishable from an
absurd vegetation. . . ."

This *creative self-consciousness* is a stage that most of us achieve
only at rare intervals; and none of us, except the saints, religious or
secular, and the great creative figures, live very much of our lives on
this level. But it is the level which gives meaning to our actions and
experiences on the lesser levels. Many people may have experienced
this consciousness in some special moment, let us say, in listening to
music, or in some new experience of love or friendship which temporarily takes them out of the usual walled-in routine of their lives. It
is as though for a moment one stood on a mountain peak, and viewed
his life from that wide and unlimited perspective. One gets his sense

* Robinson Jeffers, *op. cit.*

of direction from his view from the peak and sketches a mental map which guides him for weeks of patient plodding up and down the lesser hills when effort is dull and "inspiration" is conspicuous by its absence. For the fact that at some instant we have been able to see truth unclouded by our own prejudices, to love other persons without demand for ourselves, and to create in the ecstasy that occurs when we are totally absorbed in what we are doing—the fact that we have had these glimpses gives a basis of meaning and direction for all of our later actions.

This fourth level is what is meant in such statements as those in the Bible about losing one's life for the sake of the values one believes in. Thus it is true that there is a kind of self-forgetting on this level of consciousness. But the word self-forgetting is a poor term; this consciousness in another sense is the most fulfilled state of human existence.

One cannot *demand* the awareness we are discussing, and as we have said it often occurs in moments of receptivity and relaxation rather than action. Nonetheless the evidence in studies of creative people is that they get their important insights on those particular problems on which they have wrestled with perseverance and diligence, even though the insight itself may come at a moment of lull. One cannot *command* one's dreams, for example, but one gets fruitful insights from them to the extent that he is actively concerned with doing so, and can train himself to be vigilant in his sensitivity to his dreams.

Nietzsche described the person who has creative self-consciousness when he said about Goethe: "He disciplined himself into wholeness, he *created* himself. . . . Such a spirit who *has become free* stands amid the cosmos with a joyous and trusting fatalism, in the *faith* that . . . in the whole all is redeemed and affirmed—*he does not negate any more.*"

Part 3

✻

THE GOALS OF INTEGRATION

5

Freedom and Inner Strength

٭

WHAT would happen to a person if his freedom were entirely and literally taken away? We shall approach that question by constructing in fantasy an imaginative parable. This parable might be called

The Man Who Was Put in a Cage

One evening a king of a far land was standing at his window, vaguely listening to some music drifting down the corridor from the reception room in the other wing of the palace. The king was wearied from the diplomatic reception he had just attended, and he looked out of the window pondering about the ways of the world in general and nothing in particular. His eye fell upon a man in the square below—apparently an average man, walking to the corner to take the tram home, who had taken that same route five nights a week for many years. The king followed this man in his imagination—pictured him arriving home, perfunctorily kissing his wife, eating his late meal, inquiring whether everything was right with the children, reading the paper, going to bed, perhaps engaging in the love act with his wife or perhaps not, sleeping, and getting up and going off to work again the next day.

And a sudden curiosity seized the king which for a moment banished his fatigue, "I wonder what would happen if a man were kept in a cage, like the animals at the zoo?"

So the next day the king called in a psychologist, told him of his idea, and invited him to observe the experiment. Then the king caused a cage to be brought from the zoo, and the average man was brought and placed therein.

At first the man was simply bewildered, and he kept saying to the psychologist who stood outside the cage, "I have to catch the tram, I have to get to work, look what time it is, I'll be late for work!" But later on in the afternoon the man began soberly to realize what was up, and then he protested vehemently, "The king can't do this to me! It is unjust, and against the laws." His voice was strong, and his eyes full of anger.

During the rest of the week the man continued his vehement protests. When the king would walk by the cage, as he did every day, the man made his protests directly to the monarch. But the king would answer, "Look here, you get plenty of food, you have a good bed, and you don't have to work. We take good care of you—so why are you objecting?" Then after some days the man's protests lessened and then ceased. He was silent in his cage, refusing generally to talk, but the psychologist could see hatred glowing like a deep fire in his eyes.

But after several weeks the psychologist noticed that more and more it now seemed as if the man were pausing a moment after the king's daily reminder to him that he was being taken good care of—for a second the hatred was postponed from returning to his eyes—as though he were asking himself if what the king said were possibly true.

And after a few weeks more, the man began to discuss with the psychologist how it was a useful thing if a man were given food and shelter, and that man had to live by his fate in any case and the part of wisdom was to accept his fate. So when a group of professors and graduate students came in one day to observe the man in the cage, he was friendly toward them and explained to them that he had chosen this way of life, that there are great values in security and being taken care of, that they would of course see how sensible his course was, and so on. How strange! thought the psychologist, and how pathetic—why is it he struggles so hard to get them to approve of his way of life?

In the succeeding days when the king would walk through the

courtyard, the man would fawn upon him from behind the bars in his cage and thank him for the food and shelter. But when the king was not in the yard and the man was not aware that the psychologist was present, his expression was quite different—sullen and morose. When his food was handed to him through the bars by the keeper, the man would often drop the dishes or dump over the water and then be embarrassed because of his stupidity and clumsiness. His conversation became increasingly one-tracked: and instead of the involved philosophical theories about the value of being taken care of, he had gotten down to simple sentences like "It is fate," which he would say over and over again, or just mumble to himself, "It is."

It was hard to say just when the last phase set in. But the psychologist became aware that the man's face seemed to have no particular expression: his smile was no longer fawning, but simply empty and meaningless, like the grimace a baby makes when there is gas on its stomach. The man ate his food, and exchanged a few sentences with the psychologist from time to time; his eyes were distant and vague, and though he looked at the psychologist, it seemed that he never really *saw* him.

And now the man, in his desultory conversations, never used the word "I" any more. He had accepted the cage. He had no anger, no hate, no rationalizations. But he was now insane.

That night the psychologist sat in his parlor trying to write a concluding report. But it was very difficult for him to summon up words, for he felt within himself a great emptiness. He kept trying to reassure himself with the words, "They say that nothing is ever lost, that matter is merely changed to energy and back again." But he couldn't help feeling something *had* been lost, something had been taken out of the universe in this experiment, and there was left only a void.

Hatred and Resentment as the Price of Denied Freedom

One point in the above parable which should be especially noted is the hatred which surged up in the man when he realized he was captive. The fact that such a great amount of hatred is generated when people have to give up their freedom proves how essential a value freedom is for them. Often the person in actual life who has had to surrender much of his freedom, usually in his childhood when he could do nothing about it, and to give up some of his right and room to exist as a human being, may seem on the surface to have accepted the situation and "adjusted to" the surrender. But we do not need to penetrate far under the surface to discover that something else has come in to fill the vacuum—namely hatred and resentment of those who have forced him to give up his freedom. And usually this smoldering hatred is in direct proportion to the degree in which the person's right to exist as a human being has been taken away from him. To be sure the hatred is repressed; for the slave is not permitted to express hating thoughts toward the masters; but it is there nonetheless, and may come out, in the cases of children for example, in symptoms like the child's failing in school, or excessive physical sickness, or bed-wetting prolonged beyond the early years, and so on. Indeed it is not possible for a human being to give up his freedom without something coming in to restore the inner balance—something arising from inner freedom when his outer freedom is denied—and this something is hatred for his conqueror.

Hating or resenting is often the person's only way to keep from committing psychological or spiritual suicide. It has the function of preserving some dignity, some feeling of his own identity, as though the person—or persons, in the case of nations—were to be saying silently to their conquerors, "You have conquered me, but I reserve the right to hate you." In cases of severe neurotics or psychotics, it is often exceedingly clear that the person, driven to the wall by earlier unfortunate conditions, has kept in his hatred an inner citadel, a last vestige of dignity and pride. Like the Negro in Faulkner's novel, *Intruder in the Dust*, such contempt for the conquerors keeps the person still an identity in his own right even though outward conditions deny him the essential rights of the human being.

In cases in therapy, furthermore, where a person who has been drastically curtailed in the exercise of his powers as a human being is unable, after a period of time, to feel or bring out his hatred and resentment, prognosis is less good. Just as the capacity of the little child to stand over against his parents was essential to his being born as a free person, so the harmed person's capacity eventually to hate or feel anger is a mark of his inner potentialities for standing against his oppressors.

Another proof of the fact that if people surrender their freedom they must hate is seen in fact that totalitarian governments must provide for their people some object for the hatred which is generated by the government's having taken away their freedom. The Jews were made the scapegoat in Hitler's Germany, along with the "enemy nations," and now Stalinism has to turn the hate existing among the Russian people against the "warmongering" Western countries. As shown so vividly in the novel *1984*, if a government sets out to take away people's freedom, it must siphon off their hatred and direct it toward outside groups—otherwise the people would revolt, or go into a collective psychosis, or become psychologically "dead" and inert, no good as people or as a fighting force. This is one of the most vicious aspects of McCarthyism: it capitalizes on the impotent hatred many people in this country feel toward those who keep us in a stymied position in Korea, namely the Russian Communists, and it turns this hatred of citizens toward their fellow citizens.

We of course do not mean that hatred or resentment in themselves are good things, or that the mark of the healthy person is how much he hates. Nor do we mean that the goal of development is that everyone hate his parents or those in authority. Hatred and resentment are destructive emotions, and the mark of maturity is to transform them into constructive emotions, as we shall see below. But the fact that the human being will destroy something—generally in the long run himself—rather than surrender his freedom proves how important freedom is to him.

In Kafka's writings, as in much other modern literature, we can see the depressing picture of the modern man who has lost the capacity to stand against his accusers. The chief character in *The Trial*, K., has been arrested but he is never informed what he is guilty of. He goes from court to judge to lawyer to court again, mildly complaining and asking that someone explain to him what he is charged with, but he never asserts his rights, never draws a line saying, "Beyond this I will not retreat, whether they kill me or not." The priest's shouting at him in the church, "Don't you understand anything?"—a scream which lacked middle-class and ecclesiastical good manners but showed the profounder dignity of one person's concern for another person—has in it the meaning, "Is there no spark left within you? Can you never stand and assert yourself?" When the two executioners come for K. at the end of the novel, they offer him a knife with which to commit suicide. The crowning proof of the tragedy of a man's loss of his last vestige of dignity was that he could not even take his own life.

In conventional circles in our day one is not supposed to admit one's hatred, just as four decades ago sexual impulses were not to be admitted, and two decades ago anger and aggression were considered unseemly in good society. These negative emotions, while they could be overlooked as occasional lapses, did not fit the ideal picture of the benign, self-controlled, ever-poised, well-adjusted bourgeois citizen.

As a consequence, hatred and resentment were generally repressed. Now it is a well-known psychological tendency that when we repress one attitude or emotion, we often counterbalance it by acting or assuming an attitude on the surface which is just the opposite. You may, for example, often find yourself acting especially politely toward the person you dislike. If you are relatively free from anxiety, you may be saying to yourself in this formal politeness, quoting from St. Paul, "I treat my enemy well in order 'to heap coals of fire on his head.'" But if you are a less secure person who has had to confront more difficult problems in development, you may try to persuade yourself that you "love" this very person you hate. It is not unusual that a person who is excessively dependent upon a dominating mother or father or other authority, for example, will act toward the other as though he "loved" him to cover up his hatred. Like a boxer in a clinch, he clings to the very one who is the enemy. In real life one does not get rid of hatred and resentment this way; one generally displaces the emotions on other people, or turns them inward in self-hate.

It is thus crucial that we be able to confront our hatred openly. And it is even more essential that we face our resentment, since that is the form hatred generally takes in polite and civilized life. Most people in our society, on looking into themselves, may not be aware of any particular hatred, but they no doubt will find a good deal of resentment. Perhaps the reason that resentment is such a common, chronic and corrosive emotion in this fourth century of individual competitiveness is that hatred has been so generally suppressed.

Furthermore, if we do not confront our hatred and resentment openly, they will tend sooner or later to turn into the one affect which never does anyone any good, namely self-pity. Self-pity is the "preserved" form of hatred and resentment. One can then "nurse" his hatred, and retain his psychological balance by means of feeling sorry for himself, comforting himself with the thought of what a tough lot has been his, how much he has had to suffer—and refrain from doing anything about it.

Friedrich Nietzsche felt very bitterly and profoundly this problem of resentment in the modern period. Indeed, he again speaks from the center of modern man's psychological conflicts, for he, like so many other contemporaneous sensitive persons, rebelled against the denial of freedom but never could get fully beyond the stage of rebellion. The son of a Lutheran clergyman who died when he was a boy, brought up in a stultifying atmosphere by relatives, Nietzsche smarted under the constrictive aspects of his German background; but at the same time he always was in a struggle against it. A very religious man himself in spirit, if not in dogma, he saw the great role played by resentment in conventional morality in his society. He felt that the middle classes were shot through with suppressed resentment, and that it emerged indirectly in the form of "morals." He proclaimed that " . . . *ressentiment* is at the core of our morals," and that "Christian love is the mimicry of impotent hatred. . . ."* Anyone in our day who wishes an illustration of so-called "morality" motivated by resentment need look no farther than gossip in a small town.

---

* W. Kaufmann, *Nietzsche*, Princeton University Press, 1950, p. 91.

Even those who believe Nietzsche's view is one-sided, as it in fact is, will agree that no one can arrive at real love or morality or freedom until he has frankly confronted and worked through his resentment. Hatred and resentment should be used as motivations to re-establish one's genuine freedom: one will not transform those destructive emotions into constructive ones until he does this. And the first step is to know *whom* or *what* one hates. To take, for an example, people under dictatorial government, the first step in their revolt to regain freedom would be their shifting back their hatred to the dictatorial powers themselves.

Hatred and resentment temporarily preserve the person's inner freedom, but sooner or later he must use the hatred to establish his freedom and dignity in reality, else his hatred will destroy himself. The aim, as one person put it in a poem, is "To hate in order to win the new."

What Freedom Is Not

We can understand more clearly what freedom is if we first look at what it is not. Freedom is not rebellion. Rebellion is a normal *interim* move toward freedom: it occurs to some extent when the little child is trying to exercise his muscles of independence through the power to say "No"; it occurs more clearly when the adolescent is trying to become independent of parents. In adolescence (as possibly in other stages too) the strength of the rebelliousness against what the parents stand for is often excessive because the young person is fighting his own anxiety at stepping out into the world. When parents say "Don't" he often must scream defiance at them, because that "don't" is exactly what he feels the craven side of himself is saying, the side of himself which is tempted to take refuge behind the walls of parental protection.

But rebellion is often confused with freedom itself. It becomes a false port in the storm because it gives the rebel a delusive sense of being really independent. The rebel forgets that rebellion always presupposes an outside structure—of rules, laws, expectations— against which one is rebelling; and one's security, sense of freedom and strength are dependent actually on this external structure. They are "borrowed," and can be taken away like a bank loan which can be called in at any moment. Psychologically many persons stop at this stage of rebellion. Their sense of inner moral strength comes only from knowing what moral conventions they do not live up to; they get an oblique sense of conviction by proclaiming their atheism and disbelief.

Much of the psychological vitality of the 1920's came from rebellion. This is illustrated in the novels of F. Scott Fitzgerald, D. H. Lawrence and to some extent Sinclair Lewis. It is interesting now, when reading F. Scott Fitzgerald's *This Side of Paradise* or his other novels which were the bibles of the emancipated young people of his day, to note what a furor is made over kissing a girl, or other actions that now impress us as mere peccadillos. D. H. Lawrence carried on a great crusade in his novel *Lady Chatterley's Lover* to proclaim the thesis that Lady Chatterley, whose husband had become paralyzed, had the right to take a lover who happened to be a worker on the estate grounds. A novelist writing that novel today would scarcely find it necessary, so little does sexual freedom now have to be argued, to make the husband paralyzed.

It was not that the ideas were in themselves unworthy of serious discussion—ideas like "free love," "free expression" in bringing up children, and so on. It is that they were defined negatively, largely in terms of what one was against. We were against external compulsions on love, against rigidly curtailing the free development of children. And the emphasis, if we take the latter example, was on what the parent must *not* do—he must not interfere, and, in the extreme forms of the doctrine, the child must be allowed to do anything he wishes. It was not seen that such structureless living actually increased children's anxiety. It also was not seen that the parent must obviously take a good deal of responsibility for the child's actions, and that positive freedom consists of the parent's doing this in the context of a genuine respect for the child as a person, actually and potentially, that he give all realistic room for the potentialities of the child to develop, and that he not require the child to falsify his wants and emotions.

Those of us who were in college in the late 1920's recall what a sense of power we got from the causes and crusades, from knowing so staunchly what we were rebelling against, be it war, or sexual taboos, or companionate marriage, or booze, or prohibition or what not. But now a rebel in that sense would have a hard time getting an audience. H. L. Mencken, the great iconoclast, was the high priest of those years; and it seemed everybody on the campus read him. Who reads him now? Today this kind of rebelling is all rather boring. For when there are no set standards to rebel against, one gets no power from rebelling. It is not that the bank called in the loan: the bank simply collapsed, and no loan had any worth any more. By the middle of our century the process of demolishment begun back in the nineteenth century—a demolishment that is one side of the transformation of standards—has done its work, and we are reaping emptiness and bewilderment. "All the sad young men" like those the early F. Scott Fitzgerald wrote about got a sense of potency from kissing a girl: but since that is now "routine" and gives one no special feeling of power, these are the young men who have had to search within themselves for their potency, and in so many cases have found it lacking.

Since the rebel gets his sense of direction and vitality from attacking the existing standards and mores, he does not have to develop standards of his own. Rebellion acts as a substitute for the more difficult process of struggling through to one's own autonomy, to new beliefs, to the state where one can lay new foundations on which to build. The negative forms of freedom confused freedom with license, and overlooked the fact that freedom is never the opposite to responsibility.

Another common error is to confuse freedom with *planlessness*. Some writers these days argue that if the system of economic laissez-faire—"letting everyone do as he wishes"—were altered as history marches on, our freedom would vanish with it. The argument of these authors often goes something like this: "Freedom is like a living thing. It is indivisible. And if the individual's right to own the means of production is taken away, he no longer has the freedom to earn his living in his own way. Then he can have no freedom at all."

Well, if these writers were right it would indeed be unfortunate—for who then could be free? Not you nor I nor anyone else except a very small group of persons—for in this day of giant industries, only the minutest fraction of citizens can own the means of production anyway. Laissez-faire *was* a great idea, as we have seen, in earlier centuries: but times change, and almost everyone nowadays earns his living by virtue of belonging to a large group, be it an industry, or a university, or a labor union. It is a vastly more interdependent world, this "one world" of our twentieth century, than the world of the entrepreneurs of earlier centuries or of our own pioneer days; and freedom must be found in the context of economic community and the social value of work, not in everyone's setting up his own factory or university.

Fortunately, this economic interdependence need not destroy freedom if we keep our perspective. The pony express was a great idea, also, back in the days when sending a letter from coast to coast was an adventure. But certainly we are thankful—complain as we may about mail service these days—that now when we write a letter to a friend on the coast, we don't have to give more than a passing thought to its method of travel; we drop it in the box with an air-mail stamp and forget about it. We are free, that is, to devote more time and concern to our message to our friend, our intellectual and spiritual interchange in the letter, because in a world made smaller by specialized communication we don't have to be so concerned about how the letter gets there. We are more free intellectually and spiritually precisely because we accept our position in economic interdependence with our fellow men.

I have often wondered why there is such anxiety and such an outcry that freedom will be lost unless we preserve the old laissez-faire practices. Is not one of the reasons the fact that modern man has so thoroughly surrendered *inward* psychological and spiritual freedom to the routine of his work and to the mass patterns of social conventions that he feels the only vestige of freedom left to him is the opportunity for economic aggrandizement? Has he made the freedom to compete with his neighbor economically a last remnant of individuality, which therefore must stand for the whole meaning of freedom? That is to say, if the citizen of the suburbs could not buy a new car each year, build a bigger house, and paint it a slightly different color from his neighbor's, might he feel that his life would have no purpose, and that he would not exist as a person? The great weight placed on competitive, laissez-faire freedom seems to me to show how much we have lost a real understanding of freedom.

To be sure, freedom *is* indivisible: and this is precisely why one cannot identify it with a particular economic doctrine or *segment* of life, least of all a segment of the past; it *is* a living thing, and its life comes precisely from how the whole person relates himself to the community of his fellow men. Freedom means *openness*, a readiness to grow; it means being flexible, ready to change for the sake of greater human values. To identify freedom with a given system is to deny freedom—it crystallizes freedom and turns it into dogma. To cling to a tradition, with the defensive plea that if we lose something that worked well in the past we will have lost all, neither shows the spirit of freedom nor makes for the future growth of freedom. We shall keep faith with those courageous men, the pioneer industrialists, the men of commerce and the capitalists of the sixteenth to nineteenth centuries in the Western world, as well as with the independent frontiersmen of our own country, if we emulate their courage, dare to think boldly as they did, and plan the most effective economic measures for our day as they did for theirs.

This book is on psychology rather than economics or sociology; and we touch on the larger picture only because man always lives in a social world, and that world conditions his psychological health. We simply propose that our social and economic ideal be *that society which gives the maximum opportunity for each person in it to realize himself, to develop and use his potentialities and to labor as a human being of dignity giving to and receiving from his fellow men.* The good society is, thus, the one which gives the greatest freedom to its people—freedom defined not negatively and defensively, but positively, as the opportunity to realize ever greater human values. It follows that collectivism, as in fascism and communism, is the denial of these values, and must be opposed at all costs. But we shall successfully overcome them only as we are devoted to positive ideals which are better, chiefly the building of a society based on a genuine respect for persons and their freedom.

What Freedom Is

Freedom is man's capacity to take a hand in his own development. It is our capacity to mold ourselves. Freedom is the other side of consciousness of self: if we were not able to be aware of ourselves, we would be pushed along by instinct or the automatic march of history, like bees or mastodons. But by our power to be conscious of ourselves, we can call to mind how we acted yesterday or last month, and by learning from these actions we can influence, even if ever so little, how we act today. And we can picture in imagination some situation tomorrow— say a dinner date, or an appointment for a job, or a Board of Directors meeting—and by turning over in fantasy different alternatives for acting, we can pick the one which will do best for us.

Consciousness of self gives us the power to stand outside the rigid chain of stimulus and response, to pause, and by this pause to throw some weight on either side, to cast some decision about what the response will be.

That consciousness of self and freedom go together is shown in the fact that the less self-awareness a person has, the more he is unfree. That is to say, the more he is controlled by inhibitions, repressions, childhood conditionings which he has consciously "forgotten" but which still drive him unconsciously, the more he is pushed by forces over which he has no control. When persons first come for psychotherapeutic help, for example, they generally complain that they are "driven" in any number of ways: they have sudden anxieties or fears or are blocked in studying or working without any appropriate reason. They are unfree—that is, bound and pushed by unconscious patterns.

It may be after some months of psychotherapeutic work little changes begin to appear. The person begins to recall his dreams regularly; or in one session he takes the initiative in stating that he wants to change the subject on hand and get some help on a different problem; or one day he can say that he felt angry when the therapist said such and such; or he is able to cry when previously he never could feel much of anything, or suddenly he laughs with spontaneity and wholeheartedness, or is able to state he doesn't like Mary with whom he has been conventional friends for years but does like Carolyn. In such ways, slight as they may seem, his emerging self-awareness goes hand in hand with his enlarging power to direct his own life.

As the person gains more consciousness of self, his range of choice and his freedom proportionately increase. Freedom is cumulative; one choice made with an element of freedom makes greater freedom possible for the next choice. Each exercise of freedom enlarges the circumference of the circle of one's self.

We do not mean to imply that there are not an infinite number of deterministic influences in anyone's life. If you wished to argue that we are determined by our bodies, by our economic situation, by the fact that we happened to be born into the twentieth century in America, and so on, I would agree with you; and I would add many more ways in which we are psychologically determined, particularly by tendencies of which we are unconscious. But no matter how much one argues for the deterministic viewpoint, he still must grant that there is a *margin in which the alive human being can be aware of what is determining him*. And even if only in a very minute way to begin with, he can have some say in how he will react to the deterministic factors.

Freedom is thus shown in how we relate to the deterministic realities of life. If you set out to write a sonnet, you run up against all kinds of recalcitrant realities in the laws of rhyme and scanning, and in the necessity of fitting words together; or if you build a house, you confront all kinds of determining elements in bricks and mortar and lumber. It is essential that you know your material and accept its limits. But *what* you say in the sonnet, as Alfred Adler used to emphasize, is uniquely yours. The pattern and the style in which you build your house are products of how you, with an element of freedom, use the reality of the given materials.

The arguments of "freedom *versus* determinism" are on a false basis, just as it is false to think of freedom as a kind of isolated electric button called "free will." Freedom is shown in according one's life with realities—realities as simple as the needs for rest and food, or as ultimate as death. Meister Eckhart expressed this approach to freedom in one of his astute psychological counsels, "When you are thwarted, it is your own attitude that is out of order." Freedom is involved when we accept the realities not by blind necessity but by choice. This means that the acceptance of limitations need not at all be a "giving up," but can and should be a constructive act of freedom; and it may well be that such a choice will have more creative results for the person than if he had not had to struggle against any limitation whatever. The man who is devoted to freedom does not waste time fighting reality; instead, as Kierkegaard remarked, he "extols reality."

Let us take as an illustration a situation in which people are very much controlled, namely when they are sick with a disease like tuberculosis. In almost every action they are rigidly conditioned by the facts that they are in a sanatorium under a strict regime, have to rest such and such time, can walk only fifteen minutes a day, and so on. But there is all the difference in the world in how persons relate to the reality of the disease. Some give up, and literally invite their own deaths. Others do what they are supposed to do, but they continually resent the fact that "nature" or "God" has given them such a disease and though they outwardly obey they inwardly rebel against the rules. These patients generally don't die, but neither do they get well. Like rebels in any area in life, they remain on a plateau perpetually marking time.

Other patients, however, frankly confront the fact that they are very seriously ill; they let this tragic fact sink into consciousness through plentiful hours of contemplation as they lie in beds on the sanatorium porch. They seek in their consciousness of self to understand what was wrong in their lives beforehand that they should have succumbed to the illness. They use the cruelly deterministic fact of being sick as an avenue to new self-knowledge. These are the patients who can best choose and affirm the methods and the self-discipline— which never can be put into rules, but vary from day to day—which will bring them victoriously through the disease. They are the ones who not only achieve physical health, but who also are ultimately enlarged, enriched and strengthened by the experience of having had the disease. They affirm their elemental freedom to know and to mold deterministic events; they meet a severely deterministic fact with freedom. It is doubtful whether anyone really achieves health who does not responsibly choose to be healthy, and whoever does so choose becomes more integrated as a person by virtue of having had a disease.

Through his power to survey his life, man can transcend the immediate events which determine him. Whether he has tuberculosis or is a slave like the Roman philosopher Epictetus or a prisoner condemned to death, he can still in his freedom choose how he will relate to these facts. And *how* he relates to a merciless realistic fact like death can be more important for him than the fact of death itself. Freedom is most dramatically illustrated in the "heroic" actions, like Socrates' decision to drink the hemlock rather than compromise; but even more significant is the undramatic, steady day-to-day exercise of freedom on the part of any person developing toward psychological and spiritual integration in a distraught society like our own.

Thus freedom is not just the matter of saying "Yes" or "No" to a specific decision: it is the power to mold and create ourselves. Freedom is the capacity, to use Nietzsche's phrase, "to become what we truly are."

Freedom and Structure

Freedom never occurs in a vacuum; it is not anarchy. Earlier in this book, we pointed out how the self-consciousness of the child is born in the structure of his relations with his parents. And we emphasized that the psychological freedom of the human being develops not as though he were a Robinson Crusoe on a desert island, but in continual interaction with the other significant persons in his world. Freedom does not mean trying to live in isolation. It does mean that when one is able to confront his isolation, he is able consciously to choose to act, with some responsibility, in the structure of his relations with the world, especially the world of other persons around him.

The absurd results which can occur when the structure is not adequately emphasized are seen in some of the writings of the leader of French existentialism, Jean Paul Sartre. The chief character in Sartre's novel *Age of Reason*, apparently being portrayed as acting in freedom, actually moves along in whim and indecision, his actions motivated by the nightly recurrence of sexual desire, by his mistress' expectations of him and by other accidental external happenings. As a result one has the impression, in reading the book, of vacuity and emptiness, and one feels inclined to ask in mild boredom, "Who cares?" The mood engendered by the novel is precisely the opposite to the concern for the individual and his freedom that Sartre upholds in theory. In Sartre's drama *The Red Gloves*, the Communist hero lacks the decisiveness to fulfill his mission of assassinating the dictator, and finally is goaded into it only when he discovers his wife in the other man's arms. Hence the reviewers of the play described the hero (and I believe not unfairly) as acting like a grown-up Boy Scout with especially active sexual jealousy.

The essence of existentialism, of the Sartrian as well as other varieties, is its belief in the capacity of the individual to care greatly about his freedom and inner integrity, enough to die or commit suicide for them if need be. Sartrian existentialism was born in the resistance movement in the last war in France, in which Sartre and others fought with great courage; and it would seem that the movement borrowed much of its vitality and its structure from this fight for France's freedom. But something is wrong when such a movement becomes, as travelers from France tell us, a sophisticated fad, a rallying point for the young Parisian dilettantes.

We agree with the fundamental Sartrian precept that the individual has no recourse from the necessity of making final decisions for himself, and that his existence as a person hangs or falls in these choices; and to make them in the last analysis in freedom and isolation may require literally as well as figuratively an agony of anxiety and inward struggle. But the fact that human beings *can* choose with some freedom, and that they will at times die for this freedom (both very strange things, quite contrary to any simple doctrine of self-preservation) implies some profound things about human nature and human existence. No one will die for the negative side of a debate, or for any other negation. A person may die for a lost cause, but he is dying for very powerful positive values, such as his own dignity and integrity. The emptiness of the Sartrian viewpoint arises from the failure to analyze those very presuppositions in the freedom which he is avowedly dedicated to. One wonders what will happen to Sartre's existentialism as it gets farther away from the French resistance movement. Some astute critics have stated it may go authoritarian: Tillich believes it may go into Catholicism, and Marcel predicts it will go Marxist.

It is not our purpose here to go into detail about what specifically should be the structure of one's relations with the world. There are many different approaches. The Greeks called it "logos" (hence the term "logical"). The Stoics had the concept of "natural law," the given "form" of life by which one had to live to be happy. In the seventeenth and eighteenth centuries there was the belief in "universal reason." We only wish to emphasize that thinking persons all through the ages have sought to describe in different ways some structure: and that every individual assumes, consciously or unconsciously, some structure in which he acts. Most people tend to assume certain rules which arise from their unconscious conformity to what is expected by the society. What we have described as "conformity" and "authoritarianism" serve as the unconsciously assumed structure for many people in our day. In any case, it is better to ask one's self quite consciously what structure one assumes.

Working out an adequate view of structure is, of course, a problem for philosophy, religion and ethics working with the social sciences, including psychology. In this book we deal chiefly with psychology, and have pointed out already some of the evidence from our psychological understanding of the individual's needs and relationships which bears on the question of structure. In the succeeding chapters we shall deal more with the question of what kind of structure—in ethics, philosophy, and religion—makes for the fullest realization of the potentialities of the individual person.

"Choosing One's Self"

Freedom does not come automatically; it is achieved. And it is not gained at a single bound; it must be achieved each day. As Goethe forcefully expresses the ultimate lesson learned by Faust:

"Yes! to this thought I hold with firm persistence;
The last result of wisdom stamps it true:
He only earns his freedom and existence
Who daily conquers them anew."

The basic step in achieving inward freedom is "choosing one's self." This strange-sounding phrase of Kierkegaard's means to affirm one's responsibility for one's self and one's existence. It is the attitude which is opposite to blind momentum or routine existence; it is an attitude of aliveness and decisiveness; it means that one recognizes that he exists in his particular spot in the universe, and he accepts the responsibility for this existence. This is what Nietzsche meant by the "will to live"—not simply the instinct for self-preservation, but the will to accept the fact that one is one's self, and to accept responsibility for fulfilling one's own destiny, which in turn implies accepting the fact that one must make his basic choices himself.

We can see more clearly what choosing one's self and one's existence means by looking at the opposite—choosing not to exist, that is to commit suicide. The significance of suicide lies not in the fact that people actually kill themselves in any large numbers. It is indeed a very rare occurrence except among psychotics. But psychologically and spiritually the thought of suicide has a much wider meaning. There is such a thing as psychological suicide in which one does not take his own life by a given act, but dies because he has chosen—perhaps without being entirely aware of it—not to live. Not infrequently one hears of incidents like that in the disaster not long ago of a sinking fishing boat. A young man in his twenties clung in the choppy waters to a floating timber with an older man for an hour or so, and talked to the older man about how he felt too young to die. Finally, with the words, "I'm finished; goodbye, Pop," he let go of the timber and sank. Of course we do not know the inner psychological processes in the fact that a person, apparently with some strength left, seems to give up and die; but it is a fair guess that some inner tendency not to choose to live is in operation.

Another illustration is in the lives of persons who have dedicated themselves to certain tasks, such as taking care of a sick loved one or finishing an important work. They keep going under difficult circumstances as though they had determined they "had" to live; and then when the task is completed, when "success" is attained, they proceed to die as though by some inner decision. Kierkegaard wrote twenty books in fourteen years, completed them at the early age of forty-two, and then—we almost say "in conclusion"—he took to his bed and died.

These ways of choosing not to live show how crucial it can be to choose to live. It is doubtful whether anyone really begins to live, that is, to affirm and choose his own existence, until he has frankly confronted the terrifying fact that he could wipe out his existence but *chooses* not to. Since one is free to die, he is free also to live. The mass patterns of routine are broken: he no longer exists as an accidental result of his parents having conceived him, of his growing up and living as an infinitesimal item on the treadmill of cause-and-effect, marrying, begetting new children, growing old and dying. Since he could have chosen to die but chose not to, every act thereafter has to some extent been made possible because of that choice. Every act then has its special element of freedom.

People often actually go through the experience of committing psychological suicide in some sector of their lives. We shall present two illustrations which we hope will make the basic point clear. A woman believes she cannot live unless a certain man loves her. When he marries someone else, she contemplates suicide. In the course of her meditating on the idea for some days, she fantasies, "Well, assume I did do it." But then she suddenly thinks, "After I've done it, it would still be good to be alive in other ways—the sun still shines, water is still cool to the body, one can still make things," and the suggestion creeps in that there may still be other people to love. So she decides to live. Assuming the decision is made for positive reasons rather than just the fear of dying or inertia, the conflict may actually have given her some new freedom. It is as though the part of her which clung to the man did commit suicide, and as a result she can begin life anew. This is the increased aliveness Edna St. Vincent Millay describes in "Renascence":

> Ah, up from the ground sprang I
> And hailed the earth with such a cry
> As is not heard save from a man
> Who has been dead, and lives again.*

Or a young man feels he can never be happy unless he gains some fame. He begins to realize that he is competent and valuable, let us say as an assistant professor; but the higher he gets on the ladder the clearer he sees that there are always persons above him, that "many are called but few are chosen," that very few people gain fame anyway, and that he may end up just a good and competent teacher. He might then feel that he would be as insignificant as a grain of sand, his life meaningless, and he might as well not be alive. The idea of suicide creeps into his mind in his more despondent moods. Sooner or later he, too, thinks, "All right, assume I've done it—what then?" And it suddenly dawns on him that, if he came back after the suicide, there would be a lot left in life even if one were not famous. He then

* Lines from "Renascence" in *Renascence and Other Poems*. Published by Harper & Brothers. Copyright 1912, 1940 by Edna St. Vincent Millay.

chooses to go on living, as it were, without the demand for fame. It is as though the part of him which could not live without fame does commit suicide. And in killing the demand for fame, he may also realize as a byproduct that the things which yield lasting joy and inner security have very little to do with the external and fickle standards of public opinion anyway. He may then appreciate the more than flippant wisdom in Ernest Hemingway's remark, "Who the hell wants fame over the week-end? I want to write well." And finally, as a result of the partial suicide, he may clarify his own goals and arrive at more of a feeling for the joy which comes from fulfilling his own potentialities, from finding and teaching the truth as he sees it and adding his own unique contribution arising from his own integrity rather than the servitude to fame.

We would emphasize again that the actual process of these partial psychological suicides is much more complex than these illustrations imply. Actually some people—perhaps most people—move in the opposite direction when they have to renounce a demand: they retreat, constrict their lives and become less free. But we wish only to make clear that there is a positive aspect to partial suicide, and that the dying of one attitude or need may be the other side of the birth of something new (which is a law of growth in nature not at all limited to human beings). One can choose to kill a neurotic strategy, a dependency, a clinging, and then find that he can choose to live as a freer self. The woman in our example would no doubt find with clearer insight that her so-called love for the man for whom she would have committed suicide was really not love at all, but clinging parasitism balanced by desire to have power over the man. A "dying" to part of one's self is often followed by a heightened awareness of life, a heightened sense of possibility.

When one has consciously chosen to live, two other things happen. First, his responsibility for himself takes on a new meaning. He accepts responsibility for his own life not as something with which he has been saddled, a burden forced upon him: but as a something he has chosen himself. For this person, himself, now exists as a result of a decision he himself has made. To be sure, any thinking person realizes in theory that freedom and responsibility go together: if one is not free, one is an automaton and there is obviously no such thing as responsibility, and if one cannot be responsible for himself, he can't be trusted with freedom. But when one has "chosen himself," this partnership of freedom and responsibility becomes more than a nice idea: he experiences it on his own pulse; in his choosing himself, he becomes aware that he has chosen personal freedom and responsibility for himself in the same breath.

The other thing which happens is that discipline from the outside is changed into *self-discipline*. He accepts discipline not because it is commanded—for who can command someone who has been free to take his own life?—but because he has chosen with greater freedom what he wants to do with his own life, and discipline is necessary for the sake of the values he wishes to achieve. This self-discipline can be given fancy names—Nietzsche called it "loving one's fate" and Spinoza spoke of obedience to the laws of life. But whether bedecked by fancy terms or not, it is, I believe, a lesson everyone progressively learns in his struggle toward maturity.

6

The Creative Conscience

❈

MAN is the "ethical animal"—ethical in potentiality even if, unfortunately, not in actuality. His capacity for ethical judgment—like freedom, reason and the other unique characteristics of the human being—is based upon his consciousness of himself.

A few years ago Dr. Hobart Mowrer conducted a notable little experiment in the psychological laboratory at Harvard. The purpose was to test the "ethical" sense of rats. Could rats balance the long-term good and bad consequences of their behavior, and act accordingly? Pellets of food were dropped in a trough in front of the hungry animals, but the plan was that they should learn a kind of rat etiquette—to wait three seconds before seizing the food. If the rat didn't wait, he received a punishment in the form of an electric shock through the floor of the cage.

When the punishment occurred right after the rats had too hastily grabbed the food, they soon learned to wait "politely," and then to take their food and enjoy it in peace. That is, they could integrate their behavior around the fact "wait a moment or you'll wish you had." But when the punishment was postponed, say for nine or twelve seconds after the rats had broken the rule of etiquette, they had a very difficult time of it. Most rats could not then learn from the punishment. They became "delinquent"—that is, they grabbed the food willy-nilly, regardless of the punishment to come. Or they became "neurotic"—they withdrew from the food altogether and went hungry and frustrated. The essential point is they could not balance a *future bad* consequence of an action against their *present* desire for the food.

This little experiment highlights the difference between man and rats. Man can "look before and after." He can transcend the immediate moment, can remember the past and plan for the future, and thus choose a good which is greater, but will not occur till some future moment in preference to a lesser, immediate one. By the same token he can feel himself into someone else's needs and desires, can imagine himself in the other's place, and so make his choices with a view to the good of his fellows as well as himself. This is the beginning of the capacity, however imperfect and rudimentary it may be in most people, to "love thy neighbor" and to be aware of the relation between their own acts and the welfare of the community.

The human being not only *can* make such choices of values and goals, but he is the animal who *must* do so if he is to attain integration. For the value—the goal he moves toward—serves him as a psychological center, a kind of core of integration which draws together his powers as the core of a magnet draws the magnet's lines of force together. We pointed out in a previous chapter that knowing what one *wants* is essential for the beginnings of the child's and young person's capacity for self-direction. Knowing what one wants is simply the elemental form of what in the maturing person is the ability to choose one's own values. The mark of the mature man is that his living is integrated around self-chosen goals: he knows what he wants, no longer simply as the child wants ice cream but as the grown person plans and works toward a creative love relationship or toward business achievement or what not. He loves the members of his family not because he has been thrown together with them by the accident of birth but because he finds them lovable and chooses to love them; and he works not merely from automatic routine, but because he consciously believes in the value of what he is doing.

We saw in an earlier chapter that man's anxiety, bewilderment and emptiness—the chronic psychic diseases of modern man—occur mainly because his values are confused and contradictory, and he has no psychic core. We can now add that the degree of an individual's inner strength and integrity will depend on how much he himself believes in the values he lives by. In this chapter we inquire how a person can maturely and creatively choose and affirm such values.

In the first place, your values and mine—and our difficulty in affirming them—depend very much on the age we live in. It is always so: in an age of transition, when skepticism and doubt accompany every thought, the individual has a harder task. Goethe, who had no occasion to beat the drums for faith in the traditional sense, wrote, "All epochs that are ruled by faith, in whatever form, are glorious, elevating and fruitful in themselves and for prosperity. All epochs, on the other hand, in which skepticism in whatever form maintains a precarious triumph, even should they boast for a moment of borrowed splendor, lose their meaning . . ." because no one can take pleasure in wrestling with "what is essentially sterile."

If, in these somewhat grandiloquent words, Goethe means by faith the convictions permeating the society, giving it a center of meaning and giving to its members a sense of purpose, his statement is historically accurate. We have only to call to mind Periclean Greece, or the time of Isaiah, or Paris in the thirteenth century, or the Renaissance and seventeenth century to see how such shared convictions draw together the creative forces of the period.

But in the transitional, or disintegrating, phase of a historical period, such as at the end of the Hellenistic times and in the twilight of medievalism, the "faith" tends to break up also. Then two things generally happen. First, the beliefs and traditions handed down in the society tend to become crystallized into dead forms which suppress individual vitality. For example, the symbols used rampantly in the years of the waning of the Middle Ages became dry, empty forms, easy to argue about but devoid of content. The second thing which happens in such a time of transition is that vitality gets divorced from tradition, and tends to become diffuse rebelliousness which loses its power like water flowing in every direction on the ground. This was more or less the case in our own 1920's.

Is this not roughly our dilemma today? Are we not caught between authoritarian trends on one side and directionless vitality on the other? Whether all readers would cut the pie of history the same way I do—and certainly history can be interpreted from different angles—everyone would agree that in times of social upheaval, like our own, people suffer from feelings of "rootlessness" and tend to cling to authority and established institutions as a source of security in the storm. As Dr. and Mrs. Lynd point out in their study of the American town during the depression, in *Middletown in Transition*, "Most people are incapable of tolerating change and uncertainty in all sectors of life at once." So the citizens of Middletown were turning toward more conservative authoritarian beliefs in economics and politics, more rigid moral attitudes, and were joining in increased numbers the conservative, fundamentalistic rather than the liberal churches.

The danger in our middle of the twentieth century is that persons, confused and bewildered and at times even in panic about what to believe in (as was the case in Europe in the 1930's), will grab at destructive and demonic values. Communism comes in to fill "the vacuum of faith caused by the waning of established religion," writes Arthur M. Schlesinger, Jr. "It provides a sense of purpose which heals internal agonies of anxiety and doubt." We may not be afraid that this nation will go communistic—as I am not—but the seizing upon destructive values shows itself in other ways in our society. There are clear signs that authoritarian, reactionary trends are growing—in religion, in politics, in education, in philosophy, and in tendencies toward dogmatism in science. When people feel threatened and anxious they become more rigid, and when in doubt they tend to become dogmatic; and then they lose their own vitality. They use the remnants of traditional values to build a protective encasement and then shrink behind it; or they make an outright panicky retreat into the past.

But many are discovering that the flight to the past doesn't work. Fortunately such books as Henry Link's *Return to Religion* are as short-lived in their influence as they are temporarily popular. Such efforts are basically self-defeating: one can never apply some "center" from the outside. A resurgence of religious interest occurring as in the upset Hellenistic times because of a "failure of nerve," as Gilbert Murray put it, will do no good to the society or the persons themselves. Difficult as the task is, we must accept ourselves and our society where we are, and find our ethical center through a deeper understanding of ourselves as well as through a courageous confronting of our historical situation.

In the last few years another movement has been growing which is very different from the "return to religion." Many intellectuals and other sensitive persons have become more and more aware of their loss in being cut off from the religious and ethical traditions of the culture, and that those who were not familiar with the thought of Isaiah, Job, Jesus, Buddha, Lao-tzu were missing something of crucial significance in an age when man must rediscover his values. They have turned with a new interest to the ethical and religious wisdom of the past. Some indications of this trend are found in the articles of David Riesman, such as "Freud, Science and Religion" in *The American Scholar*, and in the writings of Hobart Mowrer. Four consecutive issues of the *Partisan Review* in 1950 were given over entirely to articles by a score of novelists, poets and philosophers on the topic "Religion and the Intellectual."

To the extent that this trend is not a product merely of the anxiety of our day—as in its best exemplars it certainly is not—it is indeed salutary. But the danger lies in the fact that some intellectuals, being newcomers to the field and therefore less able to differentiate at the moment, are apt to seize on the more obvious and vocal but less sound aspects of the religious tradition. If the interest of the intellectuals in religion chiefly contributes to the growth of authoritarianism and reaction, we are the more lost.

The real problem, thus, is to distinguish what is healthy in ethics and religion, and yields a security which increases rather than decreases personal worth, responsibility and freedom. Let us start, as we have in previous chapters, by asking how a healthy ethical awareness is born and develops in the human being.

Adam and Prometheus

Man is the ethical animal: but his achievement of ethical awareness is not easy. He does not grow into ethical judgment as simply as the flower grows toward the sun. Indeed, like freedom and the other aspects of man's consciousness of self, ethical awareness is gained only at the price of inner conflict and anxiety.

This conflict is portrayed in that fascinating myth of the first man, the Biblical story of Adam. This ancient Babylonian tale, rewritten and carried over into the Old Testament about 850 B.C., pictures how ethical insight and self-awareness are born at the same time. Like the story of Prometheus and other myths, this tale of Adam speaks a classic truth to generation after generation of people not because it refers to a particular historical event, but because it portrays some deep inward experience shared by all men.

Adam and Eve, so the story goes, live in the Garden of Eden where God "had made all sorts of trees grow that were pleasant to the sight and good for food." In this delightful land they know neither toil nor want. Even more significantly, they have no anxiety and no guilt: they "do not know they are naked." They have no struggle with the earth in wresting their living, nor psychological conflict within themselves, nor spiritual conflict with God.

But Adam had been commanded by God not to eat of the tree of the knowledge of good and evil and the tree of life in the Garden, "lest he become like God in knowing good and evil." When Adam and Eve did eat of the fruit of the first tree, "their eyes were opened"; and the first evidence of their knowing good and evil was in their experiencing anxiety and guilt. They were "aware of their nakedness," and when at noon God walked through the garden for his daily airing, as the author says in his childlike and charming style, Adam and Eve hid from his sight among the trees.

In his anger at their disobedience, God meted out punishments. The woman was condemned to have sexual cravings for her husband and to experience pain in childbirth, and to man God gave the punishment of work.

By the sweat of your brow shall you earn your living,
Until you return to the ground. . . .
For dust you are,
And to dust you must return.

This remarkable story is actually describing in the primitive way of the early Mesopotamian people what happens in every human being's development some time between the ages of one and three, namely, the emergence of self-awareness. Before that time the individual has lived in the Garden of Eden, a symbol of the period of existence in the womb and early infancy when he is entirely taken care of by parents, and his life is warm and comfortable. The Garden stands for that state reserved for infants, animals and angels, in which ethical conflict and responsibility do not exist; it is the period of innocence in which one "knows neither shame nor guilt." Such pictures of paradise without productive activity appear in many different forms in literature, and they are typically a harking back in romantic longing to the early state preceding self-awareness, or to that more extreme state with which the period of innocence has much in common psychologically, namely the existence in the womb.

With the loss of "innocence" and the rudimentary beginnings of ethical sensitivity, the myth goes on to indicate, the person falls heir to the particular burdens of self-consciousness, anxiety and guilt feeling. He likewise has an awareness—though it may not appear till later—that he is "of dust." That is to say, he realizes that he will some time die; he becomes conscious of his own finiteness.

On the positive side, this eating of the tree of knowledge and the learning of right and wrong represent the birth of the psychological and spiritual person. Indeed, Hegel spoke of this myth of the "fall" of man as a "fall upward." The early Hebrew writers who put the myth into the book of Genesis might well have made it the occasion for celestial song and rejoicing, for this is the day—rather than at the creation of Adam—when man the human being was born. But what is amazing is that all this is pictured as happening *against* God's will and commandments. God is portrayed as being angry that "man has become like one of us, in knowing good from evil; and now, suppose he were to reach out his hand and take the fruit of the tree of life also, and eating it, live forever!"

Are we to believe that this God did not wish man to have knowledge and ethical sensitivity—this God who, we are told just the chapter before in the book of Genesis, created man in his own image, which, if it means anything at all, means likeness to God in the respects of freedom, creativity and ethical choice? Are we to suppose that God wished to keep man in the state of innocence and psychological and ethical blindness?

These implications are so out of keeping with the astute psychological insight of the myth, that we must find some other explanations. To be sure, the myth, coming as it does out of that dim period of three thousand to a thousand years before Christ, represents the primitive viewpoint. It is understandable that primitive storytellers would be unable to distinguish between constructive self-consciousness and rebellion, considering the fact that many people even today find it very hard to make that distinction. Furthermore, the God in the myth is Yahweh, the earliest and most primitive Hebrew tribal deity, who is notorious as the jealous and vindictive god. It was against the cruel and unethical ways of Yahweh that the later Hebrew prophets protested.

We can get light on this strange contradiction in the Adam myth if we look at the parallel Greek myths of Zeus and the other gods on Mount Olympus which arose in the same archaic epoch. The Greek myth closest to the story of Adam is that of Prometheus, who stole fire from the gods and gave it to human beings for their warmth and productivity. The enraged Zeus, noting one night from a glow on earth that the mortals had fire, seized Prometheus, bore him off to the Caucasus, and chained him to a mountain peak. The torture devised by Zeus' skillful imagination was to have a vulture feast by day on Prometheus' liver, and then, when the liver had grown back during the night, the vulture would tear at it again the next day, thus ensuring perpetual torment for the hapless Prometheus.

So far as punishment goes, Zeus had an edge over Yahweh in cruelty. For the Greek god, smoldering in anger that man should now have fire, crammed all the diseases, sorrows and vices into a box in the form of mothlike creatures, and had Mercury take the box to the earthly paradise (very much like the Garden of Eden) in which Pandora and Epimetheus lived in untroubled happiness. When the curious woman opened it, out flew the creatures, and mankind was visited with these never-ending afflictions. These demonic elements in the gods' dealings with man certainly do not present a pretty picture.

As the Adam story is the myth of self-consciousness, Prometheus is the symbol of creativity—the bringing of new ways of life to mankind. Indeed, the name Prometheus means "forethought"—and as we have pointed out, the capacity to see into the future, to plan, is simply one aspect of self-consciousness. Prometheus' torture represents the inner conflict which comes with creativity—it symbolizes the anxiety and guilt to which—as creative figures like Michelangelo, Thomas Mann, Dostoevski and countless others have told us—the man who dares to bring mankind new forms of life is subject. But again, as in the Adam myth, Zeus is jealous of man's upward strivings and vindictive in punishment. So we are left with the same problem—what does it mean that the gods fight against man's creativity?

To be sure, there is rebellion against the gods in the actions of both Adam and Prometheus. This is the angle from which the myths as they stand make sense. For the Greeks and Hebrews knew that when a man tries to leap over his human limitations, when he commits the sin of overreaching himself (as David did in taking Uriah's wife), or commits *hubris* (as did the proud Agamemnon when he conquered Troy), or arrogates to himself universal power (as in modern fascist ideology) or holds that his limited knowledge is the final truth (as does the dogmatic person, whether he be religious or scientific), then he becomes dangerous. Socrates was right: the beginning of wisdom is the admission of one's ignorance, and man can creatively use his powers, and to some extent transcend his limitations, only as he humbly and honestly admits these limitations to begin with. The myths are sound in their warning against false pride.

But the rebellion these myths portray is clearly good and constructive at the same time; and hence they cannot be dismissed merely as pictures of man's struggle against his finiteness and pride. They portray the psychological truth that the child's "opening his eyes," and gaining self-awareness, always involves potential conflict with those in power, be they gods or parents. But why is this potential rebellion—without which the child would never acquire potentialities for freedom, responsibility, and ethical choice, and the most precious characteristics of man would lie dormant—why is this rebellion to be condemned?

We submit that in these myths there speaks the age-old conflict between entrenched authority, as represented by the jealous gods, and the upsurging of new life and creativity. The emergence of new vitality always to some extent breaks the existing customs and beliefs, and is thus threatening and anxiety-provoking to those in power as well as to the growing person himself. And those who represent the "new" may find themselves in deadly conflict with the entrenched powers—as Orestes and Oedipus found out. The anxiety in Adam and the torture experienced by Prometheus also tell us psychologically that within the creative person himself there is fear of moving ahead. In these myths there speaks not only the courageous side of man, but the servile side which would prefer comfort to freedom, security to one's own growth. The fact that in the myth of Adam and Eve the punishments meted out are *sexual desire* and *work* further proves our point. For is it not the longing to be perpetually taken care of which would lead us to conceive of work—the opportunity to till the soil and produce food, to create by the power of one's own hand—as a *punishment?* Would it not be the anxious side of one's self which would conceive of sexual desire as in itself a burden—and to castrate one's self, as Origen actually did, to avoid conflict by cutting out desire? To be sure, anxiety and guilt which accompany having to produce one's own sustenance, and the problems involved in sexual desire as well as other aspects of self-awareness, are painful. At times they certainly do bring in their train great conflict and suffering. But who would argue that, except in extreme cases such as psychosis, anxiety and guilt feelings are too great a price to pay for the venture of self-knowledge, of creativity—in short too great a price to pay for the power to be a human being rather than an innocent infant?

These myths show the authoritarian side in all religious traditions—Greek, Hebrew or Christian as it may be—which wars against new ethical insights. It is the voice of Yahweh, the jealous and vindictive God; it is the voice of the king who, jealous of his position and power, would abandon his son to the wolves, as did Oedipus' father; it is the tribal chief or priest who tends to crush the young, the new, the growing; it is the dogmatic beliefs and rigid customs which resist new creativity.

the standards by calling them "cultural" or moral rules or absolute religious doctrines, what is ethical about such conformity? Obviously such behavior leaves out the essence of human ethics—one's sensitive awareness of the unique relationship with the other person, and the working out, in some degree of freedom and personal responsibility, of the creative relationship.

One of the most remarkable pictures of the conflict between ethical sensitivity and existing institutions and of the anxiety which ethical freedom brings, is in Dostoevski's story of the Grand Inquisitor. Christ came back to earth one day, quietly and unobtrusively healing people in the streets but recognized by all. It happened to be during the Spanish Inquisition, and the old Cardinal, the Grand Inquisitor, met Christ on the street and had him taken to prison.

In the dead of night the Inquisitor comes to explain to the silent Christ why he never should have returned to earth. For fifteen centuries the church has been struggling to correct Christ's original mistake in giving man freedom, and they will not allow Him to undo their work. Christ's mistake, says the Inquisitor, was that "in place of the rigid ancient law," he placed on man the burden of having "with free heart to decide for himself what is good and what is evil," and "this fearful burden of free choice" is too much for men. Christ respected man too much, argues the Inquisitor, and forgot that actually people want to be treated as children and be led by "authority" and "miracle." He should have merely given them bread, as the devil suggested in the temptation, but "thou wouldst not deprive man of freedom and didst reject the offer, thinking, what is that freedom worth if obedience is bought with bread? . . . But in the end they will lay their freedom at our feet, and say to us, 'Make us your slaves, but feed us.' . . . Didst thou forget that man prefers peace and even death, to freedom of choice in the knowledge of good and evil?"

There are a few heroic, strong persons who could follow Christ's way of freedom, continues the old Inquisitor, but what most men seek is to be united "all in one unanimous and harmonious ant heap. . . . I tell Thee that man is tormented by no greater anxiety than to find some one quickly to whom he can hand over that gift of freedom with which the ill-fated creature is born." The church accepts the gift: "We shall allow or forbid them to live with their wives and mistresses, to have or not to have children—according to whether they have been obedient or disobedient—and they will submit to us gladly and cheerfully . . . for it will save them from the great anxiety and terrible agony they endure at present in making a free decision for themselves." The old Inquisitor, asking somewhat sadly the rhetorical question, "Why hast Thou come back to hinder our work?" states as he takes his leave that tomorrow Christ will be burned.

Dostoevski does not mean, of course, that the Inquisitor speaks for all religion, either Catholic or Protestant. He means, rather, to portray the life-thwarting side of religion which seeks the "unanimous . . . ant heap," the element in religion which enslaves the person and would tempt him to surrender, like Esau for a mess of pottage, his most precious possessions—his freedom and responsibility.

The person in our day, therefore, who seeks values around which he can integrate his living, needs to face the fact that there is no easy and simple way out. He cannot merely "return to religion" any more than he can healthily return to his parents when the freedom and responsibility of choice becomes too great a burden. For there is a double relation between ethics and religion, the same double relation we find between parents and offspring. On one hand, the ethical prophets throughout history are born and nourished in the religious tradition—one has only to call to mind Amos, Isaiah, Jesus, St. Francis, Lao-tzu, Socrates, Spinoza and countless others. But on the other hand, a bitter warfare exists between ethically sensitive people and religious institutions. Ethical insights are born in attacks upon conformity to existing mores. In the Sermon on the Mount, Jesus precedes each new ethical insight he offers with the refrain, "It was said unto you of old, but I say unto you . . ." This is the constant refrain of the man of ethical sensitivity: new wine "cannot be put into old bottles, else the bottles burst and the wine is spilt." Thus it is always: the ethically creative persons, like Socrates, Kierkegaard and Spinoza, are engaged in finding new ethical "spirit" as opposed to the formalized "law" of the traditional system.

There is always tension and sometimes even outright warfare between these ethical leaders and existing religious and social institutions, with the ethical leader often attacking the church and the church as frequently branding the other an enemy. Spinoza, the "God-intoxicated philosopher," was excommunicated; one of Kierkegaard's books is entitled *Attack on Christendom;* Jesus and Socrates were executed as "threats" to moral and social stability. It is amazing to note how often the saints of one period have been, in historical fact, the so-called atheists of the previous period.

In our own day the examples of those who attack existing religious institutions as opposed to ethical growth include Nietzsche, in his protest that Christian morality is motivated by resentment, and Freud, in his criticism of religion as ensconcing people in infantile dependency. Regardless of their theoretical beliefs, they represent the ethical concern for man's well-being and fulfillment. Though in some quarters their teachings are regarded as inimical to religion (as some of them are), I believe that in future generations the main insights of both Freud and Nietzsche will be absorbed into the ethical-religious tradition, and religion will become the richer and more effective for their contributions.

John Stuart Mill points out, for example, that his father, James Mill, considered religion the "enemy of morality." The elder Mill had been educated in a Presbyterian theological seminary in Scotland, but had later withdrawn from the church because he refused to believe that God could have created hell with the knowledge, as implied in predestination, that people were going there without their own choice. He held that religion "radically vitiated the standard of morals, making it consist of doing the will of a being, on whom it lavishes indeed all the phrases of adulation, but whom in sober truth it depicts as eminently hateful." Mill adds a point with respect to this type of "unbeliever" in the middle nineteenth century: "The best among them . . . are more genuinely religious, in the best sense of the word religion, than those who exclusively arrogate to themselves the title."*

* John Stuart Mill, *Autobiography.*

Nicolai Berdyaev, the Russian Orthodox theologian and philosopher, protests against the same sadistic doctrines as the elder Mill referred to, and also against the fact that "Christians have expressed their piety in bows, fawnings and prostrations—gestures that are symbolic of servility and humiliation." As has every ethical prophet in history, Berdyaev remarks that he would "fight against God in the name of God," and adds that it is "impossible to revolt, except with reference to and in the name of some ultimate value by which I judge that which I resolve to oppose; that is to say in the name of God . . ."*

There is a common motif in these struggles between new insight and entrenched authorities as they appear in the conflict of Adam and Yahweh, Prometheus and Zeus, Oedipus and his father, Orestes and the matriarchal powers, or in the prophets in man's actual ethical history. Is it not the same psychological motif, on a different level, as we discovered in the conflict between child and parent? *Or, more accurately, is it not the conflict between every human being's need to struggle toward enlarged self-awareness, maturity, freedom and responsibility, and his tendency to remain a child and cling to the protection of parents or parental substitutes?*

Religion—Source of Strength or Weakness?

In any discussion of religion and personality integration, the question is not whether religion itself makes for health or neurosis, but *what kind* of religion and how is it used? Freud was in error when he held that religion is per se a compulsion neurosis. Some religion is and some is not. Any area in life may be used as a compulsive neurosis: philosophy may be a flight from reality into a harmonious "system" as a protection from the anxiety and disharmonies of day-to-day life *or* it may be a courageous endeavor to understand reality better. Science may be used as a rigid, dogmatic faith by which one escapes emotional insecurity and doubt, *or* it may be an open-minded search for new truth. Indeed, since faith in science has been more

* Nicolai Berdyaev, *Spirit and Reality.* New York, Charles Scribner's Sons, 1935.

acceptable in intelligent circles in our society and therefore is less apt to be questioned, it may well be that in our day this faith more frequently plays the role of a compulsive escape from uncertainties than does religion. Freud, however, was correct technically—as he so often was—in that he asked the right question with respect to religion: does it increase dependency and keep the individual infantile?

Nor are those on the other side correct who say glibly and with comfort to the masses that religion makes for mental health. Some religion certainly does and some decidedly does not. All of these blanket statements would relieve us of the much more difficult question of penetrating to the inner meaning of the religious attitudes, and assessing them not as theoretical beliefs but as functioning aspects of the person's organic relation to his life.

The questions we propose are: Does a given individual's religion serve to break his will, keep him at an infantile level of development, and enable him to avoid the anxiety of freedom and personal responsibility? Or does it serve him as a basis of meaning which affirms his dignity and worth, which gives him a basis for courageous acceptance of his limitations and normal anxiety, but which aids him to develop his powers, his responsibility and his capacity to love his fellow men? The first issue that must be considered in answering these questions is the relation between religion and dependency.*

A mother and daughter had agreed when the daughter was very young that her life was always to be directed by the will of God. And the will of God, it was further agreed, was to be revealed to the daughter through the mother's prayers. One can well shudder to think how thoroughly this would open the girl to domination in every act and thought by her mother! How then could the girl's own capacity

---

* I use the term dependency as standing for "morbid dependency," that is, a dependency which would be fitting at a more infantile state of development but does not fit the given person's present state. Certainly dependency can be entirely normal: A one-year-old's need to be spoon-fed by its mother is normal, but an eight-year-old's need for the same treatment would not be. A ten-year-old boy's being supported by his parents is entirely constructive for his stage of development; but when a thirty-five-year-old man is supported by his parents, it is a different story. Dependency in the sense we are using it is not simply failure to grow up: it is a dynamic pattern which represents a flight from anxiety. A good synonym for dependency in the sense we are using it is "symbiosis," the condition when one organism is unable to live except as it clings to another.

to choose be anything but stifled—which the girl painfully discovered when, in her late twenties, she was caught in an insoluble dilemma because she could not make an autonomous marriage decision. This example may seem extreme, since the mother and daughter belonged to a conservative evangelical sect and the pattern is not covered over by sophisticated rationalizations. It illustrates that when a person sees himself as the mouthpiece or partner of God, as did the mother, there is no limit to the possibilities of arrogating to one's self power over others. .

This use of religion comes out frequently and vividly when a person in therapeutic sessions is struggling to establish some freedom from parental control. The parents then often, with various degrees of subtlety, make their central stand on the argument that it is the younger person's religious obligation to remain under the parents' direction, that it is in effect "God's will" that he continue under the parents' control. In letters which persons in therapy often receive from parents at such times, the parent of course quotes such Biblical passages as "Honor thy father and thy mother," rather than the later ethic of Jesus as shown in the New Testament passage we quoted above, "a man's foes shall be those of his own household."*

Most parents would insist verbally, of course, that they wish only to have the child fulfill his own potentialities. They are often quite unaware of unconscious needs to hang on to the younger person. But the fact that they so often behave *as though* the son's or daughter's fulfillment were to be achieved only by remaining under their control reveals something quite different from their conscious intentions. The son's or daughter's becoming free often stirs up some deep anxiety in the parent, an anxiety which shows how difficult it is for parents in our society really to believe in the indigenous potentialities of the child (perhaps because it is so hard for them to believe in their own potentialities), and how strong is the tendency of all entrenched authority to keep its power even at the price of "breaking" the other person into submission.

The conflicts are made more complex because the younger person

* Matthew 10:34–39.

struggling for autonomy has often been inculcated with a deep sense of doom if he does not obey parental precept. And he is already generally fighting considerable anxiety and guilt feelings within himself over his effort to be free. Often at this stage persons have dreams in which they are guilty yet not guilty—guilty like Orestes, yet having to go ahead. One such person dreamed that he was being cited as guilty by Senator McCarthy in the Senate, though he knew within himself that he really was not guilty.

The problem of being prey to someone else's power is reinforced, of course, by one's own infantile desires to be taken care of. Thus there are tendencies within one's self to give one's self over to the dominating person. About half my own psychotherapeutic work over the past ten years has been with persons from specifically religious backgrounds and in the religious professions, and about half with persons of no specific religious background or interest. I have received some impressions which, while they should be taken very tentatively, may nonetheless be helpful in illuminating some psychological effects of religious training in our society. I cite these impressions for two reasons. First, they may be useful to readers in the religious tradition who are concerned with avoiding the side of religion (as of any other part of the culture) which leads to neurotic pitfalls. Second, these impressions may be helpful to readers who are not part of any specifically religious tradition but who, like an increasing number of sensitive persons in our day, are concerned with distinguishing what aspects of religion aid in the discovery of one's personal values and what aspects do not.

These impressions are that people from religious backgrounds are apt, first, to have a more than average "zest" in wanting to do something with themselves and their lives. But, secondly, they are apt to have a particular attitude which I would call "the divine right to be taken care of." These two attitudes of course are contradictory. They are parallel to the two contradictory effects of religion which we have discussed above and will discuss later in this chapter. The first attitude—the strong interest in doing something about one's problems—needs no comment; it is a function of the person's confidence in meaning and value in life, is one constructive contribution of a mature religion and, as we shall indicate below, generally has an energizing influence on therapy.

But the attitude of "the divine right to be taken care of" is quite something else. It is one of the greatest blocks to the development of these persons toward maturity in therapy as well as in life in general. It is generally difficult for such people to see their demand to be taken care of as a problem to be analyzed and overcome, and they often react with hostility and a feeling of being "gypped" when their "right" is not honored. Of course they have been told, "God will take care of you," from the early days when they sang the song in Sunday school to the present vulgarized form of the same idea in many movies. But on a deeper level, the demand to be taken care of—particularly since hostility arises so quickly when it is frustrated—is a function of something more profound. I believe it gets its dynamic from the fact that these persons have had to give up so much. They have had to relinquish their power and their right to make moral judgments to their parents, and naturally the other half of the unwritten contract is that they then have a right to depend entirely on parental power and judgment, as a slave has a right to depend upon his master. So they *are* being gypped if the parent—or more likely the parental substitutes such as the therapist or God—does not extend them special care.

They have been taught that happiness and success would follow their "being good," the latter generally interpreted as being obedient. But being merely obedient, as we have shown above, undermines the development of an individual's ethical awareness and inner strength. By being obedient to external requirements over a long period of time, he loses his real powers of ethical, responsible choice. Strange as it sounds, then, the powers of these people to achieve goodness and the joy which goes with it are diminished. And since happiness is not the reward of virtue, as Spinoza remarked, but virtue itself, the person who surrenders his ethical autonomy has relinquished to the same degree his power to attain virtue and happiness. No wonder he feels resentful.

We can see more concretely what these people have had to give up when we look at how the "obedience morality," the emphasis on

"being good by subordinating one's self," got its power in modern culture. It takes its modern form largely from patterns copied from the
development of industrialism and capitalism in the last four centuries.
Now the subordination of the person to mechanical uniformity, the
arranging of one's life to fit the requirements of work and parsi-
mony, did bring financial and, as a result, social success during the
major part of the modern period. One could argue persuasively that
salvation follows obedience, for if one was obedient to the demands
of work in an industrial society, one tended to accumulate money.
Anyone who has read of the business acumen of the early Quakers
and Puritans, for example, knows how well these economic and moral
attitudes worked together. The "Quaker dollar" was a concrete solace
for the great resentment engendered in the middle classes because of
the emotional privations they suffered in this obedience system.

But times change, as we have indicated in earlier chapters, and in
our day "early to bed and early to rise" may make a man healthy,
but there is no guarantee that it will make him wealthy and wise.
Ben Franklin's precepts, tithing and daily fidelity to routine work, no
longer ensure success.

The religious person, furthermore, particularly if he is a minister or
otherwise engaged in professional religious work, has had to give up
a realistic attitude toward money. He is not supposed to require that
he be paid such and such a salary. In many religious circles it is considered "undignified" to talk about money, as if being paid, like toilet
activities, is a necessary part of life but the ideal is to act as though it
doesn't really occur. Labor groups, adapting to the changing economic
times of mass industry, have recognized that God does not send the
pay check by raven's mouth as food was sent to Elijah of old, and they
have learned through their unions to bring pressure to bear to get
adequate wages. But people in religious professions cannot strike for
higher wages. Instead the church is supposed to "take care of" the minister financially and otherwise; he is given discounts on the railroad
and in department stores; tuition in seminaries is lower than in other
graduate schools—all of which is not calculated to increase the minister's self-respect or others' respect for him in our particular society.

The fact that the religious person is not supposed to take active steps to ensure his financial security is another evidence of the underlying assumption in our society that material security will somehow come automatically if one is "good," an assumption closely connected with the belief that God will take care of you.

Thus it is easy to see why the person in our society who is taught to be good by subordinating himself, and only discovers sooner or later that he does not even get economic rewards for doing so, let alone happiness, should have so much resentment and anger. It is this buried resentment which gives the dynamic to the demand to be taken care of. It is as though the person were silently saying, "I was promised I would be taken care of if I was obedient: look how obedient I have been, so why am I not taken care of?"

The belief in "the divine right to be taken care of" often brings with it the feeling that one has a right to exercise power over others. That is to say, if one believes that persons should be under the power of others, he will not only submit himself to some more powerful person for the purpose of getting care, but he will feel it his "duty" to take care of—and to exercise power over—some person below him on the scale. This tendency is illustrated in its more sadistic form in the statement of one man, when questioned about his practice of controlling the younger man with whom he lived even to the extent of taking the latter's pay check every Saturday and putting him on an allowance, "Am I not my brother's keeper?"

We shall not endeavor to explain the reasons for the fact that *dominating* and *submissive* tendencies go hand in hand, and that masochism is always the reverse side of sadism. Erich Fromm has classically discussed these points in his book *Escape from Freedom*. We wish only to point out that the person who demands to be taken care of is generally endeavoring in a variety of subtle ways to get power over others at the same time. Goethe well expresses this psychological truth:

> . . . for each, incompetent to rule
> His own internal self, is all too fain to sway
> His neighbor's will, even as his haughty mind inclines.

Another tendency which is nourished by religious dependency is that of getting one's feeling of worth, prestige and power through identifying with someone else. This generally takes the form of identifying with an idealized figure of minister, priest, rabbi, bishop, or whoever above one in the hierarchy has prestige and power. Again this tendency is not confined to religion; it is present in business, politics and other aspects of community life. It is a regular phenomenon in psychotherapy called transference, and shows itself, among other ways, in the patient's needing to build the therapist up and to get prestige from the fact that the therapist is well known. But in therapy it is regarded as a problem to be eventually worked through so that the individual will come to see his therapist as the real person he is, and obtain his own feeling of worth and prestige from his own activities rather than the therapist's. This tendency in religion seems to rest on a deeper level than in some other areas of social living. It of course receives reinforcement from deteriorated interpretations of "vicarious suffering" and "atonement." It is as though everyone were trying to live vicariously through someone else, until no one knows where he himself is. It is amazing how easily the Christian teaching of love can deteriorate into everyone's agreeing, "If you take responsibility for me, I will for you."

The neurotic uses of religion have one thing in common: they are devices by which the individual avoids having to face his loneliness and anxiety. God is made into a "cosmic papa," in Auden's phrase. Religion in this form is a rationalization for covering up the realization—a realization which contains a good deal of terror for those who take it seriously—that the human being is in the depths of himself basically alone, and that there is no recourse from the necessity of making one's choices ultimately alone.

> . . . it is utter
> Terror and loneliness
> That drive a man to address the Void as 'Thou.'*

* Lines from *Conversation at Midnight*. Published by Harper & Brothers. Copyright 1937 by Edna St. Vincent Millay.

Thus speaks a character in Edna St. Vincent Millay's *Conversation at Midnight*. But if the need to escape terror and loneliness are the main motives for turning to God, one's religion will not help him toward maturity or strength; and it will not even give him security in the long run. Paul Tillich, writing from the theological view, makes the point that despair and anxiety can never be worked through until one confronts them in their stark and full reality. This truth is obviously just as valid psychologically. Maturity and eventual overcoming of loneliness are possible only as one courageously accepts his aloneness to begin with.

It often occurs to me that the reason Freud was able to work with such courage and unswerving purpose throughout the last forty years of his life was that he won the battle of being able to grow and work alone in that first solitary ten years, when, after he had separated from Breuer, he pursued his explorations into psychoanalysis with neither colleague nor co-worker. It seems to me, further, that this is the battle the creative ethical figures like Jesus win in the wilderness, that the real meaning of the temptations with which Jesus wrestled was not in the desire for bread or power, but in the temptation, as put in the words of the devil in the story, to throw himself down from the mountain to prove that God was protecting him:

> He will give his angels charge of you;
> they will bear you on their hands,
> lest you strike your foot against a stone.

When one has been able to say "No" to the need that he be "borne up," when, in other words, he is able not to demand he be taken care of, when he has the courage to stand alone, he can then speak as one with authority. And did not Spinoza's refusing to flee from excommunication by his church and community mean his winning the same inner battle of integrity, the same struggle for the power not to be afraid of aloneness, without which the noble *Ethics*, certainly one of the great works of all time, could not have been written?

However these thoughts may be, Spinoza gives us a statement

which blows like a fresh and cleansing wind through the foggy, morbid swamps of clinging dependency in religion: "Whoso loveth God truly must not expect to be loved by Him in return." Here speaks, in this shattering sentence, the brave man—the man who knows that virtue *is* happiness, not a claim check for it; that the love of God is its own reward, that beauty and truth are to be loved because they are good, and not because they will redound to the credit of the artist or scientist or philosopher who loves them.

Spinoza of course does not at all mean to imply the martyr-like, sacrificial, masochistic attitude for which his sentence might be mistaken. He rather is stating in its most unequivocal form the basic characteristic of the objective, mature, creative person (in his words the blessed and joyful person), namely the capacity to love something for its own sake, not for the sake of being taken care of or gaining a bootlegged feeling of prestige and power.

Certainly loneliness and anxiety can be constructively met. Though this cannot be done through the *deus ex machina* of a "cosmic papa," it can be achieved through the individual's confronting directly the various crises of his development, moving from dependence to greater freedom and higher integration by developing and utilizing his capacities, and relating to his fellows through creative work and love.

This does not imply that there is no such thing as authority in religion or any other field. It does imply that the question of authority should first be put the other way around, that is, as the question of personal responsibility. For authoritarianism (the neurotic form of authority) grows in direct proportion to the degree in which the individual is trying to avoid responsibility for meeting his problems himself. In therapy, for example, it is precisely the times when the patient feels some special or overpowering anxiety that he seeks to make an authority of the therapist. And the fact that at these times he tends to identify the therapist with God and his parents presents another proof for the contention above: that he is searching for someone to whom he can hand himself over for care. Fortunately it is not difficult to demonstrate that the therapist is not God—and it is a red-letter day in a patient's therapy when he discovers this fact and is not frightened. Instead of trying to argue with one's self or others on the merits of various authorities, therefore, it is better initially to confront one's self, in self-scrutiny, with the question: "What anxiety makes me now wish to run to the wings of an authority, and what problem of my own am I trying to evade?"

The upshot of this discussion is that religion is constructive as it strengthens the person in his sense of his own dignity and worth, aids him in his confidence that he can affirm values in life, and helps him in the use and development of his own ethical awareness, freedom and personal responsibility. Thus religious faith or practices like prayer cannot be called "good" or "bad" in themselves. The question is, rather, how much the belief or practice is, for the given person, an escape from his freedom, a way of becoming "less" of a person; or how much it is a way of strengthening him in the exercise of his own responsibility and ethical power. The person praised in Jesus' parable in Matthew was not the one who was afraid and "buried" his talent, but the persons who courageously used their talents; and these, the "good and faithful" persons, were given more power.

The Creative Use of the Past

In the final paragraph of his last book,* the venerable Freud quotes this verse from Goethe:

What thou has inherited from thy fathers,
Acquire it to make it thine.

We now consider how a person can acquire the inheritance from his fathers in the ethical and religious tradition. We have placed this section after the one above, for it makes no sense to talk about tradition until the problem of dependency is clarified. To the extent that an adult person has achieved some freedom and identity as a self, he has

* *An Outline of Psychoanalysis.*

a base from which to acquire the wisdom in the past traditions of his society and to make it his. But if this freedom is missing, traditions block rather than enrich. They may become an internalized set of traffic rules, but they will have little or no fructifying influence on one's inward development as a person.

As we saw in Chapter 2, part of the malady of our day is that we have lost much of our creative relationship to the wisdom of the past. Henry Ford's statement in the 1920's, "History is bunk," received wide publicity and occasioned a good deal of debate. The mere fact that such an issue could ever be accepted for discussion indicates the rebelliousness toward tradition which was fairly prevalent then. But history is our social, communal body: in it we live, move and have our being; and to cut one's self off from it, to hold it is inconsequential, is about as sensible as to say, "My physical body is bunk."

To be proud of having no interest in the religious traditions of one's society falls in the same category. In the 1920's and even later to an extent, it has often been the attitude among sophisticated people that to have no concern with religious tradition was a sign of emancipation. Indeed, educated people who would be ashamed to admit knowing nothing about economics or literature have been proud of illiteracy in the field of religion—or proud of the fact that they have learned no more than the odd assortment of fiction and catechism they got in early years in Sunday school. The attitudes of dependency which we discussed in the previous section and these sophisticated attitudes both have the same result: they shut the person off from a creative relationship to an important segment of the "wisdom of thy fathers." This situation is unfortunate not only for the society but also for the person himself. For it robs him of an important part of his historical body, and thus contributes much to the diffuse perplexity and feelings of rootlessness of individuals in our day.

It is important, therefore, whether we are "intellectuals" or "sophisticates" or merely alert human beings seeking bearings in a confused and perplexed time, to ask, How can one relate to the inherited traditions so that one's own freedom and personal responsibility are not sacrificed in the process?

One principle, to start with, is clear: *the greater a person's aware-*

ness of himself, the more he can acquire the wisdom of his fathers to make it his. It is the persons who are weak in the sense of their own personal identity who are overcome by the power of tradition, who cannot stand in its presence, and who therefore either capitulate to it, cut themselves off from it, or rebel against it. This is graphically illustrated by some modern artists who are afraid to look at Renaissance pictures for fear they might be influenced. One of the distinguishing marks of strength as a self is the capacity to immerse one's self in tradition and at the same time be one's own unique self.

This is what the classics, in literature or ethics or any other field, should do for one. For the essence of a classic is that it arises from such profound depths in human experience that, like the works of Isaiah, or *Oedipus*, or *The Way* of Lao-tzu, it speaks to us who live centuries later in vastly different cultures as the voice of our own experience, helping us to understand ourselves better and enriching us by releasing echoes within ourselves which we may not have known were there. "Deep calleth unto deep," as the psalmist puts it. One need not go along literally with Jung's concept of archetypes or "the collective unconscious" to agree that the deeper one goes into one's own experience (let us say in confronting death, or experiencing love, or in the elemental relations in the family), the more one's experience has in common with similar experiences of other men in other ages and cultures. This is why the dramas of Sophocles, the dialogues of Plato, and the paintings of reindeer and bison on the cave walls in Southern France by anonymous Cro-Magnon men some twenty-thousand years ago may speak more powerfully and elicit greater response in us than the bulk of the writings or pictures of five years ago.

But the more profoundly one delves into his own experience, the more original are his reactions and productions. Here is the seeming paradox, which no doubt everyone knows to be true in his own experience, that *the more profoundly he can confront and experience the accumulated wealth in historical tradition, the more uniquely he can at the same time know and be himself.*

The battle, therefore, is not between individual freedom and tradition as such. The issue, again, is how the tradition is used. If a person asks, "What does the tradition (be it a tradition in ethics like the Ten Commandments or the Sermon on the Mount or a tradition in art like impressionism) require of me?" he is turning tradition to authoritarian uses. Tradition will then not only quench his own vitality and creative insight, but it will also serve as a convenient way for him to avoid responsibility for his own choices. But if he asks, "What does the tradition have to teach me about human life, in my particular time and with my problems?" he is using the wealth of wisdom accumulated through historical tradition for his own enrichment and guidance as a free person.

One of the first things necessary for a creative relationship to the inherited wisdom in the religious traditions is to remove religious discussion from such deteriorated forms as the debates over the "belief in the existence of God." The tendency to make that issue central—as though God were an "object" alongside other objects, whose existence can be proved or disproved as we prove or disprove a mathematical proposition or a scientific fact—shows our modern tendency to split up reality. And then, following the dichotomy which Descartes bequeathed to us, we tend to assume that everything must be proven by the methods which properly fit mechanics and physical science.

To make God an entity, a being over against other beings, located in space heaven only knows where, is a carry-over of a primitive view, full of contradictions and easily refutable. Paul Tillich, in a recently published book which scholars are already referring to as probably the most important theological work so far in the twentieth century, points out that to argue *for* the existence of God implies as much atheism as to argue *against* it. "It is as atheistic to affirm the existence of God as to deny it. God is being itself, not *a* being."*

We define religion as the assumption that life has meaning. Religion, or lack of it, is shown not in some intellectual or verbal formulations but in one's total orientation to life. Religion is whatever the individual takes to be his ultimate concern. One's religious attitude is to be found at that point where he has a conviction that there are values in human existence worth living and dying for.

* Paul Tillich, *Systematic Theology.* University of Chicago Press, 1951.

We obviously do not mean that all religious traditions or attitudes are equally constructive: they may be destructive, as illustrated in the religious fervor of the Nazis, or in the Inquisition. The problem always remains for theology, philosophy and ethics, with the aid of the sciences and history of man, to determine what beliefs are most constructive and most consistent with other truth about human life. The point we wish to emphasize is that psychologically religion is to be understood as a way of relating to one's existence. "By their fruits ye shall know them." Erich Fromm is entirely accurate when he remarks, "There is much less difference between a mystic's faith in God [by which he means the indigenous convictions of the religious person rather than other-worldly creeds] and an atheist's rational faith in mankind than between the former and that of a Calvinist whose faith in God is rooted in the conviction of his own powerlessness and in his fear of God's power."*

When one is able to relate creatively to the wisdom of his fathers in the ethical and religious tradition he finds that he discovers anew his capacity for *wonder*. It is self-evident that the capacity for active, responsive wonder has been largely lacking in modern society. This is one side of the vacuity and emptiness which so many people feel in our period.

Wonder may be described in many ways, from Kant's statement, "Two things incline the heart to wonder, the moral law within and the starry sky above" (and on the latter point Freud agreed), to the wonder which grips us as one aspect of the feelings of pity and terror which purge the soul, as Aristotle pointed out, when we see dramatic tragedy. Though certainly not the exclusive province of religion, wonder is traditionally associated with it: and I would consider wonder, when it appears as is so often the case in scientists or artists, as the religious aspect of these other vocations. Those who take a rigid view either of religious or scientific truth become more dogmatic and lose the capacity to wonder; those who "acquire the wisdom of their fathers" without surrendering their own freedom find that wonder adds to their zest and their conviction of meaning in life.

* *Man For Himself,* Rinehart & Company, p. 210.

The importance of wonder underlies Jesus' high regard for the attitudes of children: "Except ye become as a little child, ye cannot enter the Kingdom of Heaven." This statement has nothing whatever to do with "childishness" or "infantilism"; it refers to the child's capacity for wonder, a capacity found likewise in the most mature and creative adults, whether they are scientists like Einstein or artists like Matisse. Wonder is the opposite to cynicism and boredom; it indicates that a person has a heightened aliveness, is interested, expectant, responsive. It is essentially an "opening" attitude—an awareness that there is more to life than one has as yet fathomed, an experience of new vistas in life to be explored as well as new profundities to be plumbed. Nor is it an easy attitude to hold. "The faculty of wonder tires easily," writes Joseph Wood Krutch. ". . . Life would seem a great deal fuller than it does if it were not for the fact that the human being is, by nature, a creature to whom 'O altitudo' is much less natural than 'so what!'"

Wonder is a function of what one holds to be of ultimate meaning and value in life. Though it may be cued off by a tragic drama, it is not a negative experience; since it is essentially an enlarging of life, the over-all emotion which accompanies wonder is joy. "The highest to which man can attain is wonder," remarked Goethe; "and if the prime phenomenon makes him wonder, let him be content; nothing higher can it give him. . . ."

Wonder also goes with humility—not the pseudo-humility of submission, which generally is the reverse side of arrogance, but the humility of the generous-minded person who can accept the "given" just as he, in his own creative efforts, is able to give. The historical term "grace" has a rich meaning at this point, despite the fact that for many people the word has been so much identified with deteriorated forms of the "grace of God" that it is useless. One speaks of the graceful flight of a bird, the grace of a child's movements, the graciousness of the generous person. Grace is something "given," a new harmony which emerges; and it always "inclines the heart to wonder."

We must emphasize that in every use of these terms—wonder, humility, grace—the connotation is not that of the person being passive and acted upon, as in some traditional religious attitudes. There is a very common misconception in our society that one "gives oneself over" to creative ecstasy, or to the loved one, or to religious belief. It is as though one "falls" in love by way of gravitation, or is seized by the "hounds of heaven," or writes music or paints in a state of "being carried away." It is amazing both how prevalent these passive ways of thinking are in our culture, and how false they are. Any artist or writer or musician—those who are supposedly "carried away"—will tell you that in the creative experience there is a greatly heightened consciousness and very intense activity on his own part. To use the sexual relationship as a simile, it is as though one were to think of having intercourse by "giving himself over," without erection, without motion, and thus without interrelatedness with the other. Such passivity is equally ineffective in sexual relationships as in other creative activities. Even responsiveness implies aliveness. The music of a Kreisler makes no difference to one who is drunk or shut off in his own pride, or in other ways atrophied. And certainly the grace, or given quality of any experience is in direct proportion to how much one participates in it. A patient in therapy expressed it simply but beautifully, "The grace of God is the capacity to change."

The approach we are here recommending as the creative use of tradition makes possible a new attitude toward *conscience*. As everyone knows, conscience is generally conceived of as the negative voice of tradition speaking within one—the "thou-shalt-not's" echoing down from Moses on Mount Sinai, the voice of the prohibitions which the society has taught its members for centuries. Conscience is then the constrictor of one's activities.

This tendency to think of conscience as that which tells the individual *not* to do things, is so strong that it seems to operate almost automatically. When I was discussing this point with a class of students in a college, one student volunteered that it is quite possible to use one's conscience positively. When I agreed and asked him for examples, he offered, "When you don't want to go to class, your conscience tells you to." I pointed out that this actually was a negative sentence. He then searched his mind and came up with a second example, "When you don't want to study, your conscience makes you." He was at first entirely unaware that this example too was negative. Conscience in each case was seen as acting *against* what one supposedly "wants" to do; it was the taskmaster, the whip. The significant point is that the young man said nothing about conscience in his examples as a guide to help him get the most value from the class, or conscience as the voice of his own deepest purposes and goals in the enterprise of studying and learning.

Conscience is not a set of handed-down prohibitions to constrict the self, to stifle its vitality and impulses. Nor is conscience to be thought of as divorced from tradition, as in the liberalistic period when it was implied that one decided every act *de novo. Conscience, rather, is one's capacity to tap one's own deeper levels of insight, ethical sensitivity and awareness, in which tradition and immediate experience are not opposed to each other but interrelated.* The etymology of the term reveals this point. Composed of the two Latin words meaning "to know" (*scire*) and "with" (*cum*), conscience is very close to the term consciousness. In fact in some countries, such as Brazil, the same word ("*consciencia*") is used both for "conscience" and "consciousness." When Fromm speaks of conscience as "man's recall to himself," the recall is not opposed to historical tradition as such, but only to the authoritarian uses of tradition. For there is a level on which the individual participates in the tradition, and on that level tradition aids man in finding his own most meaningful experience.

We wish thus to emphasize the positive aspects of conscience—conscience as the individual's method of tapping wisdom and insight within himself, conscience as an "opening up," a guide to enlarged experience. This is what Nietzsche was referring to in his paean on the theme "*beyond* good and evil," and what Tillich means in his concept of the *trans*moral conscience. With this view it will no longer be true that "conscience doth make cowards of us all." Conscience, rather, will be the taproot of courage.

The Person's Power to Do the Valuing

Some readers may have been thinking, during our discussion of the loss of the center of values in our society, that what is necessary is simply to work out a new set of values. And others may have the thought, "There's nothing wrong with the values of the past—such as love, equality and human brotherhood. We need simply to bring these values back again."

Both of these points miss the central problem—namely, that modern man has to a great extent lost the power to affirm and believe in *any* value. No matter how important the content of the values may be, or how suitable this or that value may be on paper, what the individual needs is a prior capacity, namely, the *power to do the valuing*. The triumph of barbarism in such movements as Hitlerian fascism did not occur because people "forgot" the ethical traditions of our society as one might misplace a code. The humanistic values of liberty and the greatest good for the greatest number, the Hebrew Christian values of community and love for the stranger, were still in the textbooks, were still taught in Sunday school, and no archeological expedition was needed to unearth them. People rather have lost—for the reasons we discussed in Chapter 2—the inner capacity to *affirm*, to experience values and goals as real and powerful for themselves.

There is, furthermore, something artificial about setting out to "find" a center of value, as though one were shopping for a new coat. The endeavors to discover values outside one's self generally slide the individual directly into the question of what the group expects of him—what is the "style" these days, in values as in coats? And this, as we have seen, has been part-and-parcel of the trends toward emptiness in our society.

There is even something wrong in the phrase "discussion of values." One never receives his convictions about values through intellectual debates. The things in a person's life which he actually does value—his children and his love for them and theirs for him, the pleasure he has in drama or listening to music or playing golf, the pride he has in his work—all these he accepts as realities. He would regard any theoretical discussion of the value of his loving his children, or his pleasure in music, for example, as irrelevant if not impertinent. If you pushed him, he would say, "I value the love of my children because I actually *experience* it," and if you pressed far enough to irritate him, he might well say, "If you haven't experienced it your-self, I can't explain it to you." In actual life the real value is something we experience as connected with the reality of our activity, and any verbal discussion is on a quite secondary level.

We do not mean to "psychologize" values, or to imply that any-thing toward which one is inclined at the moment is "good" and "true." Nor are we implying any depreciation of the role of the sci-ences of man, as well as philosophy and religion, in clarifying values. Indeed, I believe that the combined contributions of all these disci-plines are required for the solution of our crucial problem of what values modern man can live by.

But we do mean to emphasize that unless the individual himself can affirm the value; unless his own inner motives, his own ethical awareness, are made the starting place, no discussion of values will make much real difference. Ethical judgment and decision must be rooted in the individual's own power to evaluate. Only as he himself affirms, on all levels of himself, a way of acting as part of the way he sees reality and chooses to relate to it—only thus will the value have effectiveness and cogency for his own living. For this obviously is the only way he can or will take responsibility for his action. And it is the only way that he will *learn* from his action how better to act next time, for when we act by rote or rule we close our eyes to the nuances, the new possibilities, the unique ways in which every situation is different from every other. Furthermore, it is only as the person chooses the action, affirms the goal in his own awareness, that his action will have conviction and power, for only then will he really believe in what he is doing.

Man should really be called "the valuator," said the old Zara-thustra. "No people could live without first valuing; if a people will maintain itself, however, it must not value as its neighbor valueth. . . . Valuing is creating; hear it, ye creating ones! Valuation itself is the treasure and jewel of the valued things. Through valuation only is there value; and without valuation the nut of existence would be hollow. Hear it, ye creating ones!"

Let us see more concretely *how* a man makes an ethical choice.

Every act has an infinite number of deterministic elements in it, to be sure, but at the moment of personal decision something occurs which is not just the product of these conditioning forces.

A man, for example, is confronted with a picket line as he arrives to board a steamer for a trip to fill a speaking engagement. The strike, say, is one in which the issue of justice is far from simple, as in the recent disputes in the New York harbor between two stevedore unions. The man is confronted with what for him, let us assume, is a strong ethical issue—shall he cross the picket line? He may endeavor by countless means to determine the justice of the strike, to weigh his own needs to take the trip, or alternate means of transportation. But at the point of decision to board the ship or not, he draws himself together and *assumes the risk in his decision*. This risk will be present no matter which way he decides. The action, like a dive into the water, is done by the person as a whole or not at all. To be sure we are speaking in somewhat ideal terms; many persons would tend to act by a rule—"I never cross picket lines," or "The hell with strikers"—and to rationalize out of the responsibility this way or that. But to the extent that the person is able to fulfill his human capacities in any action—that is, to choose in self-awareness—he makes the decision as a relative unity. This element of unity does not arise merely out of the integration of his personality—though the more mature he is, the more will he be able to act in this way. Rather, it arises from the fact that any action chosen in self-awareness is a placing of one's self on "the line" as it were; it involves a commitment, to a greater or lesser extent a "leap." It is as though one were saying, "To the best of my lights at the moment this is what I choose to do, even though I may know more and choose differently tomorrow."

The person's act of choosing itself throws a new element into the picture. The configuration is changed, if ever so slightly; someone has thrown his weight on one side or the other. This is the creative and the dynamic element in decision.

As everyone knows, a person is influenced in a multitude of ways by "unconscious" forces. But it is often overlooked that conscious decisions, if they are soundly and not precipitately or defiantly made, can change the direction in which unconscious forces push. This is illustrated most fascinatingly in dreams in therapeutic sessions when a person has been struggling for months to make the decision, let us say, to leave home and get a job on his own. During these months his dreams have been roughly equally on the pro and con side of the issue, some dreams warning him to stay home, others saying it is better to go. He finally makes the decision to leave, and his dreams suddenly become strongly on the positive side, as if the conscious decision releases some "unconscious" power likewise.* It seems that there are potentialities within us for health which are not released until we make a conscious decision. Allegorically, the individual's decision is like that of the Israelites in their battle against the army of Sisera: "the stars in their courses fought against Sisera," but not until the Israelites decided to fight, too.

An ethical act, then, must be an action chosen and affirmed by the person doing it, an act which is an expression of his inward motives and attitudes. It is honest and genuine in that it would be affirmed in his dreams as well as his waking thoughts. Thus an ethical man does not act on the conscious level as though he loves someone when on unconscious levels he hates him. To be sure, no integrity is perfect; all human actions have some ambivalence, and no motives are entirely pure. An ethical action does not mean one must act as a *completely* unified person—with no doubts at all—or one would never act. One will always have struggle, doubt, conflict. It means only that one has endeavored to act as nearly as possible from the "center" of himself, that he admits and is aware of the fact that his motives are not completely clear and assumes responsibility for making them clearer as he learns in the future.

In this emphasis on inner motives in ethical acts, the findings of modern psychotherapy and the ethical teachings of Jesus have their clearest parallel. For the essential point in Jesus' ethics was

---

* Of course there may also be a reaction—a slightly different pattern which does not refute our point above. Generally the reaction is severe, however, only when the person has made a decision too quickly, that is, before he was ready on all levels to do so.

his shifting the emphasis from the *external* rules of the Ten Commandments to *inward* motives. "Out of the heart are the issues of
life." The ethical issues of life, he held, are not simply "thou shalt not
kill," but rather are inward attitudes toward other persons—anger,
resentment, exploitative "lust in the heart," "railings," "jealousies,"
and so on. The wholeness of the man whose external actions are at
one with his inner motives is what is meant by the expression in
the beatitudes, the "pure in heart." Thus Kierkegaard entitles one of
his little books *Purity of Heart Is to Will One Thing*, a discussion
of a Biblical quotation which he translates, "Purify your hearts, ye
double-minded!"

Some persons will be frightened by the freedom in such an ethics of inwardness, and made anxious by the responsibility which
this places on each man's decisions. They may yearn for the "rules,"
the absolutes, the "rigid ancient law," as the Inquisitor put it, which
relieves us of "this fearful burden of free choice." And in the longing for a rule, one might protest, "Your ethics of inward motives
and personal decision lead to anarchy—everyone can then act as he
wishes!" But freedom cannot be avoided by such an argument. For
what is "honest" and "true" for a given person is not totally dis-
similar from what is true for others. Dr. Tillich has stated that "the
principles which constitute the universe must be sought in man," and
the converse is true, that what is found in man's experience is to some
extent a reflection of what is true in the universe.

This can be clearly illustrated in art. A picture is never beautiful if
it is not honest, and to the extent that it is honest, that is, represents
the immediate, deep and original perceptions and experience of the
artist, it will have at least the beginnings of beauty. This is why the
art work of children, when it is an expression of their simple and
honest feelings, is almost always beautiful: any line one makes as a
free, spontaneous person will have in it the beginning of grace and
rhythm. The harmony, balance and rhythm which are principles of
the universe, present in the movement of stars as well as atoms, and
underlying our concepts of beauty, are likewise present in the harmony of rhythm and balance of the body as well as other aspects of

the self. But at the moment the child begins to copy, or to draw to get praise from adults, or to draw by rules, the lines become rigid, constricted, and the grace vanishes.

The truth in the "inner light" tradition in religious history is that one must always begin with himself. "No one has known God," said Meister Eckhart, "who has not known himself—fly to the soul, the secret place of the Most High." Relating this truth to Socrates, Kierkegaard writes, "In the Socratic view each individual is his own center, and the entire world centers in him, because his self-knowledge is a knowledge of God." This is not the whole story of ethics and the good life, but certainly if we do not start there we will get no place.

7

Courage, the Virtue of Maturity

❄

IN any age courage is the simple virtue needed for a human being to traverse the rocky road from infancy to maturity of personality. But in an age of anxiety, an age of herd morality and personal isolation, courage is a *sine qua non*. In periods when the mores of the society were more consistent guides, the individual was more firmly cushioned in his crises of development; but in times of transition like ours, the individual is thrown on his own at an earlier age and for a longer period.

It may seem curious to devote a chapter to courage, since our tendency in the past decades was generally to relegate courage to the shelf of the old-fashioned virtues of knighthood, or at most to admit it as necessary for adolescents in sport or for soldiers in war. But we could bypass courage only because we oversimplified life: we suppressed our awareness of death, told ourselves that happiness and freedom would come automatically and assumed that loneliness, anxiety and fear were always neurotic and could be overcome by better adjustment. It is true that neurotic anxiety and loneliness can and should be overcome: the chief courage needed in dealing with them is in taking steps to get professional help. But there still remain the experiences of normal anxiety which confront any developing person, and it is in confronting rather than fleeing these that courage is essential. Courage is the basic virtue for everyone so long as he continues to grow, to move ahead; it is, as Ellen Glasgow remarks, "the only lasting virtue."

We do not refer chiefly to the courage needed to face external threats, such as war and the H-bomb. We refer rather to courage as an inward quality, a way of relating to one's self and one's possibilities. As this courage in dealing with one's self is achieved, one can with much greater equanimity meet the threats of the external situation.

Courage to Be One's Self

Courage is the capacity to meet the anxiety which arises as one achieves freedom. It is the willingness to differentiate, to move from the protecting realms of parental dependence to new levels of freedom and integration. The need for courage arises not only at those stages when breaks with parental protection are most obvious—such as at the birth of self-awareness, at going off to school, at adolescence, in crises of love, marriage and the facing of ultimate death—but at every step in between as one moves from the familiar surroundings over frontiers into the unfamiliar. "Courage, in its final analysis," as the neuro-biologist Dr. Kurt Goldstein well puts it, "is nothing but an affirmative answer to the shocks of existence, which must be borne for the actualization of one's own nature."

The opposite to courage is not cowardice: that, rather, is the lack of courage. To say a person is a coward has no more meaning than to say he is lazy: it simply tells us that some vital potentiality is unrealized or blocked. The opposite to courage, as one endeavors to understand the problem in our particular age, is automaton conformity.

The courage to be one's self is scarcely admired as the top virtue these days. One trouble is that many people still associate that kind of courage with the stuffy attitudes of the self-made men of the late nineteenth century, or with the somewhat ridiculous no matter how sincere "I-am-the-master-of-my-fate" theme in such a poem as "Invictus." With what qualified favor many people today view standing on one's own convictions is revealed in such phrases as "sticking one's neck out." The central suggestion in this defenseless posture is that any passer-by could swing at the exposed neck and cut off the head. Or people describe moving ahead in one's beliefs as "going out on a limb." Again what a picture! The only things one can do out on a limb are to crawl back again, saw the limb off and come down, dramatic as Icarus in a martyr-like and probably useless crash, or remain out on the limb, vegetating like a Hindu tree-sitter and exposed to the ridicule of a populace which does not think highly of tree-sitting, till the limb breaks off of its own dead weight.

Both of these expressions highlight the fact that what is most dreaded is getting out of the group, "protruding," not fitting in. People lack courage because of their fear of being isolated, alone, or of being subjected to "social isolation," that is, being laughed at, ridiculed or rejected. If one sinks back into the crowd, he does not risk these dangers. And this being isolated is no minor threat. Dr. Walter Cannon has shown in his study of "voodoo death," that primitive people may be literally killed by being psychologically isolated from the community. There have been observed cases of natives who, when socially ostracized and treated by their tribes as though they did not exist, have actually withered away and died. William James, furthermore, has reminded us that the expression "to be cut *dead*" by social disapproval has much more truth than poetry in it. It is thus no figment of the neurotic imagination that people are deathly afraid of standing on their own convictions at the risk of being renounced by the group.

What we lack in our day is an understanding of the friendly, warm, personal, original, constructive courage of a Socrates or a Spinoza. We need to recover an understanding of the positive aspects of courage— courage as the inner side of growth, courage as a constructive way of that becoming of one's self which is prior to the power to give one's self. Thus, when in this chapter we emphasize standing on one's own belief, we do not at all imply living in a vacuum of separateness; actually, courage is the basis of any creative relationship. To take an illustration from the sexual aspect of love: we have seen that many of the problems of disturbed potency among men are due to a fear of women by way of fear of their mother, a focus of anxiety which may be symbolically expressed by their fear of the penis being absorbed and taken away during invagination, fear of the woman's domination, or of becoming dependent on her, and so on. In therapy the origins of these problems have to be worked through quite specifically. But when this is accomplished, and the neurotic anxiety is overcome, courage then must go along with the capacity to relate, and this courage, to continue our sexual example, is literally as well as symbolically shown in the capacity for erection and the assertion necessary for active intercourse. The sexual analogy holds true for other relations of life: *it takes courage not only to assert one's self but to give one's self.*

From the time of the ancient story of Prometheus onward, it has been recognized that to create requires courage. Balzac, who well knew this truth from his own experience, has so vividly described this kind of courage that we let his words speak for us:

The quality that above all deserves the greatest glory in art—and by that word we must include all creations of the mind—is courage; courage of a kind of which common minds have no conception, and which is perhaps described here for the first time. . . . To plan, dream, and imagine fine works is a pleasant occupation to be sure. . . . But to produce, to bring to birth, to bring up the infant work with labor, to put it to bed full-fed with milk, to take it up again every morning with inexhaustible maternal love, to lick it clean, to dress it a hundred times in lovely garments that it tears up again and again; never to be discouraged by the convulsions of this mad life, and to make of it a living masterpiece that speaks to all eyes in sculpture, or to all minds in literature, to all memories in painting, to all hearts in music—that is the task of execution. The hand must be ready at every moment to obey the mind. And the creative moments of the mind do not come to order. . . . And work is a weary struggle at once dreaded and loved by those fine and powerful natures who are often broken under the strain of it. . . . If the artist does not throw himself into his work like a soldier into the breach, unreflectingly; and if, in that crater, he does not dig like a miner buried under a fall of rock . . . the work will never be completed; it will perish in the studio, where production becomes impossible, and the artist looks on at the suicide of his own talent. . . . And it is for that reason that the same reward, the same triumph, the same laurels, are accorded to great poets as to great generals.*

We now know through psychoanalytic studies, as Balzac did not, that one of the reasons creative activity takes so much courage is that to create stands for becoming free from the ties to the infantile past, breaking the old in order that the new can be born. For creating external works, in art, business or what not, and creating one's self—that is, developing one's capacities, becoming freer and more responsible—are two aspects of the same process. Every act of genuine creativity means achieving a higher level of self-awareness and personal freedom, and that, as we have seen in the Promethean and Adam myths, may involve considerable inner conflict.

A landscape painter, whose main problem was freeing himself from ties to a possessive mother, had for years wanted to paint portraits but had never dared. Finally pulling his courage together, he "dove" in and painted several portraits in the course of three days. They turned out to be excellent. But, strangely enough, he felt not only considerable joy but strong *anxiety* as well. The night of the third day he had a dream in which his mother told him he must commit suicide, and he was calling up his friends to say good-bye with a terrifying and overwhelming sense of loneliness. The dream was saying in effect, "If you create, you will leave the familiar, and you will be lonely and die; better to stay with the familiar and not create." It is highly significant, when we see the nature of this powerful unconscious threat, that he could paint no more portraits for a month—until, that is, he had overcome the counterattack of the anxiety which had appeared in the dream.

In Balzac's beautiful statement there is one point with which we would disagree, that is, "common minds have no conception" of this

* Honoré de Balzac, *Cousin Bette*. New York, Pantheon Books, pp. 236–8.

courage. This is the error which comes from identifying courage with obviously spectacular acts like the soldier's charge or Michelangelo's struggles in completing the paintings on the ceiling of the Sistine Chapel. With our present knowledge of the unconscious working of the mind, we know that struggles requiring courage equal to that of the soldier's charge take place in almost anyone's dreams and deeper conflicts in times of difficult decision. To reserve courage for "heroes" and artists only shows how little one knows of the profundity of almost any alive human being's inner development. Courage is necessary in every step in a person's movement from the mass—symbolically the womb—to becoming a person in his own right; it is at each step as though one suffers the pangs of his own birth. Courage, whether the soldier's courage in risking death or the child's in going off to school, means the power to *let go* of the familiar and the secure. Courage is required not only in a person's occasional crucial decision for his own freedom, but in the little hour-to-hour decisions which place the bricks in the structure of his building of himself into a person who acts with freedom and responsibility.

Thus we are not talking about heroes. Indeed, obvious heroism, such as rashness, is often the product of something quite different from courage: in the last war the "hot" pilots in the air force who appeared to be very brave in taking risks were often the ones who were unable to overcome their anxiety inwardly and had to compensate for it by courting danger in external rash deeds. Courage must be judged as an inner state; otherwise external actions can be very misleading. Galileo compromised externally with the Inquisition and agreed to recant his view that the earth moves round the sun. But what is significant is that he remained inwardly free, as is shown in his aside, according to legend, "It still does move round the sun." Galileo was able to go on working: and no one from the outside can say for another what decisions constitute a giving up or a preserving of freedom. We could imagine that the temptation to escape from freedom might have been present in a voice within Galileo, "Just refuse to agree—meet a martyr's death, and think of the relief from having to continue to make these new scientific discoveries!"

For it requires greater courage to preserve inner freedom, to move on in one's inward journey into new realms, than to stand defiantly for outer freedom. It is often easier to play the martyr, as it is to be rash in battle. Strange as it sounds, steady, patient growth in freedom is probably the most difficult task of all, requiring the greatest courage. Thus if the term "hero" is used in this discussion at all, it must refer not to the special acts of outstanding persons, but to the heroic element potentially in every man.

Is not all courage basically moral courage? What is generally called physical courage, meaning the capacity to risk physical pain, may be simply a difference in physical sensitivity. Whether children or adolescents have the courage to fight depends only minorly on the pain involved. It depends rather on whether the child dares risk parental disapproval, or whether he can bear the added isolation of having enemies, or whether the role he has unconsciously assumed for himself as a way of getting his security is standing up for himself or endeavoring to be liked by being compliant and "playing weak." Persons who have been able to fight wholeheartedly and without inner conflict report that generally the physical pain is overcome by the zest of the conflict. And is not the so-called physical courage of risking death really a moral courage—the courage to commit one's self to a value greater than one's existence as such, and thus the courage to let go of one's life if need be?

In my clinical experience, the greatest block to a person's development of courage is his having to take on a way of life which is not rooted in his own powers. We can see this point in the case of a young man who came for therapy because of homosexual tendencies, great feelings of anxiety and isolation, and rebellious tendencies which regularly disrupted his work. As a child he had been regarded as a sissy and could never fight despite being attacked by schoolmates almost daily. He had been the youngest child of six, there being four older brothers and, directly above him, a sister. The sister died in early childhood, and the mother, who had passionately wanted a girl after the four sons, was inconsolable. She then became very close to this youngest boy and began to treat and dress him like a girl. For him to develop feminine interests, not to learn sports with other boys, not to fight even though he was offered financial rewards by his elder brothers if he would do so, were quite logical developments: *he must not risk his position with his mother.* For it was clear that acceptance and approval could be gained if he accepted the proffered role of a girl—but where would he be as a fifth son? His mother already unconsciously rejected him because he was not in fact a girl; if he acted like a boy, he would be hated by her as a symbol that she had no girl and as a reminder that the little girl had died. These requirements, obviously contrary to his innate male tendencies, led to great resentment, hatred, and later rebellion—none of which he could dare express toward his mother. The basis for his development of courage as a male had been taken out from under him. As an adult he now showed great courage in socially rebellious acts; if a revolt against male authority was called for, he leapt into the fray. But he was terrified when any issue arose of his standing against any older woman, that is, any mother substitute—his actual mother having by this time died. What could not be risked was the final disapproval by and isolation from the mother image in his own mind.

Thus a person is unable to know *what* he believes, let alone stand up for it, or what his own powers are, if he has had all along to live up to some role of himself in his parents' eyes—an image he carries on and perpetuates within himself. His courage is a vacuum before he ever begins to act, since it has no real basis within himself.

Normally a child can take each step in differentiation from his parents, each step in becoming himself, without unbearable anxiety. Just as he learns to climb the steps despite the pain and frustration of falling back time and again, and eventually succeeds with a laugh of joy, so he normally feels out his own psychological independence step by step. Aware of his parents' love, and aware of a security present in proportion to his degree of immaturity, he can take the occasional crises with parents and such crises as going to school, and his growing courage is not overwhelmed. He is not required to stand alone to a greater degree than he is prepared to do. But if the parents need, like the mother above, to force the child into a role or dominate or overprotect the child out of their own anxiety, his task is made that much more difficult.

Parents who have inner, often unconscious, doubts about their own strength tend to demand that their children be especially courageous, independent and aggressive; they may buy the son boxing gloves, push him into competitive groups at an early age, and in other ways insist that the child be the "man" they inwardly feel they are not. Generally parents who push the child, like those who overprotect him, are showing in actions which speak louder than words their own lack of confidence in him. But just as no child will develop courage by being overprotected, so no child will develop it by being pushed. He may develop obstinacy or bullying tendencies. But his courage grows only as an outcome of his confidence, generally unverbalized, in his own powers and his indigenous qualities as a human being. This confidence gets its base from his parents' love for him and their belief in his potentialities. What he needs is neither overprotection nor pushing, but help to utilize and develop his own power, and most of all to feel that his parents see him as a person in his own right and love him for his own particular capacities and values.

Only rarely, of course, do parents require that the child assume the role of the opposite sex. Much more often their requirements are that the child fulfill the social amenities of the parents' social group, get good grades and be elected to societies in college, be "normal" in every respect so he never will be talked about, marry a suitable mate or go on in father's business. And when the son or daughter conforms to these requirements, even though, let us say, they do not believe in them, they generally rationalize their actions by saying they need to keep parental support, financial and otherwise. But on a deeper level there is usually another motive which is even more relevant to the problem of courage. That is, living up to parental expectations is the way to gain admiration and praise from the parents, and to continue as the "apple of the parental eye." Thus vanity and narcissism are the enemies of courage.

We define vanity and narcissism as the compulsive need to be praised, to be liked: for this people give up their courage. The vain and narcissistic person seems on the surface to overprotect himself, not to take any risks and in other ways to act as a coward because he thinks too highly of himself. Actually, however, just the opposite is the case. He has to preserve himself as a commodity by which he can buy the praise and favor he needs, precisely because without mother's or father's praise he would feel himself to be worthless. Courage arises from one's sense of dignity and self-esteem; and one is uncourageous because he thinks too poorly of himself. The persons who require that others continually say, "He is so nice," or so intelligent or good, or "She is so beautiful," are persons who take care of themselves not for the reason that they love themselves, but because the beautiful face or the clever mind or the gentlemanly behavior is a means of purchasing the parental pat on the head. This leads to a contempt for one's self: and thus many gifted persons whose qualities have made them lauded in the public eye will confess in the confidence of therapy that they feel like fakers.

Vanity and narcissism—the compulsive needs to be admired and praised—undermine one's courage, for one then fights on someone else's conviction rather than one's own. In the Japanese movie *Rashomon*, the husband and robber fight with complete abandon when they themselves have chosen to fight. But in another scene, when the wife screams taunts at them, and they fight because of their compulsion to live up to her requirement of their masculine prowess, they fight with only half their strength: they strike the same blows, but it is as though an invisible rope held back their arms.

When one acts to gain someone else's praise, furthermore, the act itself is a living reminder of the feeling of weakness and worthlessness: otherwise there would be no need to prostitute one's attitudes. This often leads to the "cowardly" feeling which is the most bitter humiliation of all—the humiliation of having co-operated knowingly in one's own vanquishment. It is not so bad to be defeated because the enemy is stronger, or even to be defeated because one didn't fight; but to know one was a coward because one chose to sell out his strength to get along with the victor—this betrayal of one's self is the bitterest pill of all.

There are also specific reasons in our culture why acting to please others undermines courage. For such acting, at least for men, often means playing the role of one who is unassertive, unaggressive, "gentlemanly," and how can one develop power, including sexual potency, when he is supposed to be unassertive? With women, too, these ways of gaining admiration militate against the development of their indigenous potentialities, for their potentialities are never exercised or even brought into the picture.

The hallmark of courage in our age of conformity is the capacity to stand on one's own convictions—not obstinately or defiantly (these are expressions of defensiveness not courage) nor as a gesture of retaliation, but simply because these are what one believes. It is as though one were saying through one's actions, "This is my self, my being." Courage is the *affirmative* choice, not a choice because "I can do no other"; for if one can do no other, what courage is involved? To be sure, at times one has simply to cling with dogged determination to a position he has won through courage. Such times are frequent in therapy when a person has achieved some new growth and must then withstand the counterattack of anxious reaction within himself as well as the attacks of friends and family members who would be more comfortable if he had remained the way he was. There will be plenty of defensive actions at best; but if one has conquered something worth defending, then one defends it not negatively but with joy.

When in a person's development courage begins to emerge—that is, when the person begins to break out from the pattern of devoting his life to getting others to admire him—an intermediate step generally occurs. The persons in this stage take independent stands, to be sure, but they defend their actions at the court in which the laws are written by the very authorities they have been trying to please. It is as though they demanded the right to be free, but, like the American colonists before the Revolution, they have to argue their case on the basis of laws written by those from whom they demand their rights. People in therapy in this stage often dream literally of trying to persuade their parents of the justice of their cause, of their "right" to be themselves. It may well be that this stage is the farthest that many people reach in their development toward freedom and responsibility.

But in the final analysis this halfway station leaves the person in a hopeless dilemma: for in granting his parents or parental substitutes the right to draft the laws, and in arguing before their court, he has already tacitly admitted their sovereignty. This implies his lack of freedom, and his guilt if he asserts his freedom. We have already seen that this was the dilemma of the hero in Kafka's novel *The Trial*, who was always caught because he tried to argue his case on the assumption of the complete authority of his accusers. He was then in a hopelessly frustrating position, and was reduced, quite logically, to a position in which he could only beg from them. Imagine what would have occurred if Socrates at his trial had tried to argue against his Athenian accusers on the basis of their assumptions, their laws. All the difference in the world is made by his presupposition, "Men of Athens, I will obey God rather than you," which, as we have seen above, meant for him finding his guides for conduct in the innermost center of himself.

The hardest step of all, requiring the greatest courage, is to deny those under whose expectations one has lived the right to make the laws. And this is the most frightening step. It means accepting responsibility for one's own standards and judgments, even though one knows how limited and imperfect they are. This is what Paul Tillich means by the "courage to accept one's finiteness"—which, he holds, is the basic courage every man must have. It is the courage to be and trust one's self despite the fact that one is finite; it means acting, loving, thinking, creating, even though one knows he does not have the final answers, and he may well be wrong. But it is only from a courageous acceptance of "finitude," and a responsible acting thereon, that one develops the powers that one does possess—far from absolute though they be. To do this presupposes the many sides of the development of consciousness of self which we have discussed in this book, including self-discipline, the power to do the valuing, the creative conscience, and the creative relation to the wisdom of the past. Obviously this step requires a considerable degree of integration, and the courage it requires is the courage of maturity.

A Preface to Love

We shall not go into the specific subject of love in very great detail, both because the topic has been referred to at countless points all through this book, and because the real problem for people in our day is preparatory to love itself, namely to become *able* to love. To be capable of giving and receiving mature love is as sound a criterion as we have for the fulfilled personality. But by that very token it is a goal gained only in proportion to how much one has fulfilled the prior condition of becoming a person in one's own right. Thus this whole book, not just this section, might be called a "preface to love."

In the first place it should be noted that love is actually a relatively rare phenomenon in our society. As everyone knows, there are a million and one kinds of relationships which are *called* love: we do not need to list all of the confusions of "love" with sentimental impulses and every kind of oedipal and "back to mother's arms" motifs as they appear in the romantic songs and the movies. No word is used with more meanings than this term, most of the meanings being dishonest in that they cover up the real underlying motives in the relationship. But there are many other quite sound and honest relationships called love—such as parental care for children and vice versa, or sexual passion, or the sharing of loneliness; and again the startling reality often discovered when one looks underneath the surface of individuals' lives in our lonely and conformist society, is how little the component of love is actually involved even in these relationships.

Most human relationships, of course, spring from a mixture of motives and include a combination of different feelings. Sexual love in its mature form between a man and woman is generally a blend of two emotions. One is "eros"—the sexual drive toward the other, which is part of the individual's need to fulfill himself. Two and a half millennia ago Plato pictured "eros" as the drive of each individual to unite with the complement to himself—the drive to find the other half of the original "androgyne," the mythological being who was both man and woman. The other element in mature love between man and woman is the affirmation of the value and worth of the other person, which we include in our definition of love given below.

But granted the blending of motives and emotions, and granted that love is not a simple topic, the most important thing at the outset is to call our emotions by their right names. And the most constructive place to begin learning how to love is to see how we fail to love. We shall have made a start, at least, when we recognize our situation as that of the young man in Auden's *The Age of Anxiety:*

So, learning to love, at length he is taught
To know he does not.

Our society is, as we have seen, the heir of four centuries of competitive individualism, with power over others as a dominant motivation; and our particular generation is the heir of a good deal of anxiety, isolation and personal emptiness. These are scarcely good preparations for learning how to love.

When we look at the topic on the level of national relations, we come to similar conclusions. It is easy enough to slide into the comforting sentiment, "Love will solve all." To be sure, it is obvious that this distraught world's political and social problems cry out for the attitudes of empathy, imaginative concern, love for the neighbor and "the stranger." Elsewhere I have pointed out that what our society lacks is the experience of community, based on socially valuable work and love—and lacking community we fall into its neurotic substitute, the "neurosis of collectivism."* But it is not helpful to tell people, *ipso facto*, that they should love. This only promotes hypocrisy and sham, of which we have a good deal too much in the area of love already. Sham and hypocrisy are greater deterrents to learning to love than is outright hostility, for at least the latter may be honest and can then be worked with. Simply the proclaiming of the point that the world's hostilities and hatreds would be overcome if only people could love invites more hypocrisy; and furthermore, we have learned in our dealings with Russia how crucial it is to lead from strength, and to meet authoritarian sadism directly and realistically. Certainly every new act in international relations which affirms the values and needs

* See Rollo May, *The Meaning of Anxiety*. New York, Ronald Press, 1950, Chapter 5.

of other nations and groups, as did the Marshall Plan, should be welcomed with rejoicing. At least we are learning at long last that we must affirm other nations' existence for our own sheer survival. But though such lessons are great gains, we cannot thereby conclude that occasional actions of this kind are a proof that we have learned—on the political level—to love. So, again, we shall make our most useful contribution to a world in dire need of concern for the neighbor and stranger if we begin by trying to make ourselves as individuals able to love. Lewis Mumford has remarked, "As with peace, those who call for love loudest often express it least. To make ourselves capable of loving, and ready to receive love, is the paramount problem of integration; indeed the key to salvation."

So great is the confusion about love in our day that it is even difficult to find agreed upon definitions of what love is. We define love as *a delight in the presence of the other person and an affirming of his value and development as much as one's own.* Thus there are always two elements to love—that of the worth and good of the other person, and that of one's own joy and happiness in the relation with him.

The capacity to love presupposes self-awareness, because love requires the ability to have empathy with the other person, to appreciate and affirm his potentialities. Love also presupposes freedom; certainly love which is not freely given is not love. To "love" someone because you are not free to love someone else, or because you happen by the accident of birth to be in some family relation to him, is not to love. Furthermore, if one "loves" because one cannot do without the other, love is not given by choice; for one could not choose not to love. The hallmark of such unfree "love" is that it does not discriminate: it does not distinguish the "loved" person's qualities or his being from the next person's. In such a relation you are not really "seen" by the one who purports to love you—you might just as well be someone else. Neither the one who loves nor the loved one act as *persons* in such relationships; the former is not a subject operating with some freedom, and the latter is significant chiefly as an object to be clung to.

There are all kinds of dependence which in our society—having so many anxious, lonely and empty persons in it—masquerade as love. They vary from different forms of mutual aid or reciprocal satisfaction of desires (which may be quite sound if called by their right names), through the various "business" forms of personal relationships to clear parasitical masochism. It not infrequently happens that two persons, feeling solitary and empty by themselves, relate to each other in a kind of unspoken bargain to keep each other from suffering loneliness. Matthew Arnold describes this beautifully in *Dover Beach:*

> Ah, love, let us be true
> To one another! for the world, which seems
> To lie before us like a land of dreams,
> So various, so beautiful, so new,
> Hath really neither joy, nor love, nor light,
> Nor certitude, nor peace, nor help for pain;
> And we are here as on a darkling plain. . . .

But when "love" is engaged in for the purpose of vanquishing loneliness, it accomplishes its purpose only at the price of increased emptiness for both persons.

Love, as we have said, is generally confused with dependence: but in point of fact, you can love only in proportion to your capacity for independence. Harry Stack Sullivan has made the startling statement that a child cannot learn "to love anybody before he is pre-adolescent. You can get him to sound like it, to act so you can believe it. But there is no real basis and if you stress it you get queer results, many of which become neuroses."* That is to say, until this age the capacity for awareness and affirmation of other persons has not matured enough for love. As an infant and child he is quite normally dependent on his parents, and he may in fact be very fond of them, like to be with them, and so forth. Let parents and children frankly enjoy the happiness such a relationship makes possible. But it is very healthy

* In Dr. Sullivan's paper in *Culture and Personality,* ed. Sargent and Smith, New York, 1949, p. 194.

and relieving for parents, in the respect of reducing their need to play god and their tendency to arrogate to themselves complete importance in nature's scheme for the child's life, to note how much more spontaneous warmth and "care" the child shows in dealing with his teddy bear or doll or, later on, his real dog than he shows in his relations with human beings. The bear or doll make no demands on him; he can project into them all he likes, and he does not have to force himself beyond his degree of maturity to empathize with their needs. The live dog is an intermediate step between the inanimate objects and human beings. Each step—from dependence, through dependability to interdependence—represents the developmental stage of the child's maturing capacity for love.

One of the chief things which keeps us from learning to love in our society, as Erich Fromm and others have pointed out, is our "marketplace orientation." We use love for buying and selling. One illustration of this is in the fact that many parents expect that the child love them as a repayment for their taking care of him. To be sure, a child will learn to pretend to certain acts of love if the parents insist on it; but sooner or later it turns out that a love demanded as a payment is no love at all. Such love is a "house built upon sand" and often collapses with a crash when the children have grown into young adulthood. For why does the fact that the parent has supported or protected a child, sent him to camp and later to college, have anything necessarily to do with his loving the parent? It could as logically be expected that the son should love the city traffic policeman on the corner who protects him from trucks or the army mess sergeant who gets him his food when he is in the army.

A deeper form of this demand is that the child should love the parent because the parent has sacrificed for him. But sacrifice may be simply another form of bargaining and may have nothing to do in motivation with an affirmation of the other's values and development.

We receive love—from our children as well as others—not in proportion to our demands or sacrifices or needs, but roughly in proportion to our own capacity to love. And our capacity to love depends, in turn, upon our prior capacity to be persons in our own right. To love means, essentially, to give; and to give requires a maturity of self-feeling. Love is shown in the statement of Spinoza's we have quoted above, that truly loving God does not involve a demand for love in return. It is the attitude referred to by the artist Joseph Binder: "To produce art requires that the artist be able to love—that is to give without thought of being rewarded."

We are not talking about love as a "giving *up*" or self-abnegation. One gives only if he has something to give, only if he has a basis of strength within himself from which to give. It is most unfortunate in our society that we have had to try to purify love from aggression and competitive triumph by identifying it with weakness. Indeed, this inoculation has been so much of a success that the common prejudice is that the weaker people are, the more they love; and that the strong man does not *need* to love! No wonder tenderness, that yeast without which love is as soggy and heavy as unrisen bread, has been generally scorned, and often separated out of the love experience.

What was forgotten was that tenderness goes along with strength: one can be gentle as he is strong; otherwise tenderness and gentleness are masquerades for clinging. The Latin origin of our words is nearer the truth—"virtue," of which love is certainly one, comes from the root *vir*, "man" (here in the sense of masculine strength), from which the word "virility" is also derived.

Some readers may be questioning, "But does one not *lose* himself in love?" To be sure, in love as in creative consciousness, it is true that one is merged with the other. But this should not be called "losing one's self"; again like creative consciousness, it is the highest level of fulfillment of one's self. When sex is an expression of love, for example, the emotion experienced at the moment of orgasm is not hostility or triumph, but *union* with the other person. The poets are not lying to us when they sing of the ecstasy in love. As in creative ecstasy, it is that moment of self-realization when one temporarily overleaps the barrier between one identity and another. It is a giving of one's self and a finding of one's self at once. Such ecstasy represents the fullest interdependence in human relations; and the same paradox applies as in creative consciousness—one can merge one's self in ecstasy only as one has gained the prior capacity to stand alone, to be a person in one's own right.

We do not mean this discussion to be a counsel of perfection. Nor is it meant to rule out or depreciate all of the other kinds of positive relationships, such as friendship (which may also be an important aspect of parent-child relations), various degrees of interchange of human warmth and understanding, the sharing of sexual pleasure and passion, and so on. Let us not fall into the error so common in our society of making love in its ideal sense all-important, so that one has only the alternatives of admitting he has never found the "pearl of great price" or resorting to hypocrisy in trying to persuade himself that all of the emotions he does feel are "love." We can only repeat: we propose calling the emotions by their right names. Learning to love will proceed most soundly if we cease trying to persuade ourselves that to love is easy, and if we are realistic enough to abandon the illusory masquerades for love in a society which is always talking about love but has so little of it.

Courage to See the Truth

In one of his flashing aphorisms which illuminate a whole new landscape like a burst of lightning, Nietzsche proclaimed, "Error is cowardice!" That is to say, the reason we do not see truth is not that we have not read enough books, or do not have enough academic degrees, but that we do not have enough courage.

By "truth" we do not mean scientific facts alone, or even chiefly. The problem with facts is to be accurate. If you recall the last dozen questions which troubled you—on which, that is, you had to ponder and "chew" to find out what you could believe was true—you will discover that very few if any of them had to do with matters that could be proven by scientific facts. Which job to take, whether one is in love or not, how to help one's child with a social problem in school, or what one feels or wants in this matter or that—it is such questions that occupy one during the day and even during his dreams at night. Technical proofs rarely help one on such issues. One has to venture, and whether one arrives at the best answer depends very intimately on the degree of one's maturity and courage. Even in discovering scientific truth before it is reduced to accepted formulae, such as Columbus' venture to prove the earth was round or Freud's early explorations, the finding of the truth hinges greatly on the investigator's inner qualities of probity and courage.

A graphic picture of the inner struggle required to see truth is given us in a letter the philosopher Schopenhauer wrote to Goethe. Telling of his travails in working out his thoughts after their conception, Schopenhauer writes, ". . . then I stand before my own soul, like an inexorable judge before a prisoner lying on the rack, and make it answer until there is nothing left to ask. Almost all the errors and unutterable follies of which doctrines and philosophies are so full seem to me to spring from a lack of this probity. The truth was not found, not because it was unsought, but because the intention always was to find again instead some preconceived opinion or other, or at least not to wound some favorite idea, and with this aim in view subterfuges had to be employed against both other people and the thinker himself. It is the courage of making a clean breast of it in the face of every question that makes the philosopher. He must be like Sophocles' Oedipus, who, seeking enlightenment concerning his terrible fate, pursues his indefatigable inquiry even when he divines that appalling horror awaits him in the answer. But most of us carry in our hearts the Jocasta, who begs Oedipus for God's sake not to inquire further; and we give way to her, and that is the reason why philosophy stands where it does. . . . The philosopher [must] interrogate himself without mercy. This philosophical courage, however, does not arise from reflection, cannot be wrung from resolutions, but is an inborn trend of the mind."

We agree with Schopenhauer—as does the psychoanalyst Ferenczi when he quotes this letter—that such probity is necessary if one is to see truth, and that it does not come from the intellect as such but is a part of the inborn capacity for self-awareness. We do not agree, however, that it is an "inborn trend" in the respect that one can do nothing about it. Such probity is an ethical attitude, involving courage and other aspects of one's relation to one's self; it not only *can* be developed to an extent but *must* be developed if a person is to fulfill himself as a human being.

Schopenhauer well refers to King Oedipus as his illustration of the tremendous courage necessary to see truth, and the statements of Jocasta, the wife and mother, as the temptations to avoid seeing truth. Oedipus, determined to clear up the terrible mystery that he suspects surrounds his birth, calls in the old shepherd who had many years before been ordered to kill him as a newborn baby. The shepherd is the one man who can solve the question as to whether Oedipus has really married his mother. In the words in Sophocles' drama, Jocasta tries to dissuade Oedipus:

> . . . Best take life easily,
> As a man may. . . .
> Why ask who 'twas he spoke of?
> Nay, never mind—never remember it—

When Oedipus persists she cries,

> Don't seek it! I am sick, and that's enough! . . .
> Wretch, what thou art O might'st thou never know!

But Oedipus is not to be put off by her hysteria:

> I will not hearken—not to know the whole. . . .
> Break out what will, I shall not hesitate,
> Low though it be, to trace the source of me.

When the shepherd cries,

> O, I am at the horror, now, to speak!

Oedipus rejoins:

> And I to hear. But I must hear—no less.

When Oedipus learns the horrible truth that he has killed his father and married Jocasta, his mother, he puts his eyes out. This is a very important symbolic act—"self-blinding" is literally what people do when they have profound inner conflicts. They blind themselves so that they are closed off in greater or less degree from the reality around them. Since Oedipus does this after learning how he has been living a delusion, we may take it as an act symbolizing the tragic difficulty, the "finiteness" and "blindness" of man in seeing the truth about himself and his origin.

Oedipus' situation may seem extraordinary, but the difference between his struggle in seeing truth and ours in the common run of life is one of degree, not kind. The drama gives us an age-old but ever new picture of the inner pain and conflict in finding out truths about ourselves. It is this aspect of the drama, rather than the fact that Oedipus slept with his mother, which makes Freud's selection of the myth a stroke of genius. For to seek truth is always to run the risk of discovering what one would hate to see. It requires that kind of relationship to one's self, and that confidence in ultimate values, that one can dare to risk the possibility of being uprooted from the beliefs and day-to-day values by which one has lived. It is not surprising, then, as Pascal has remarked, that "a genuine love of wisdom is a relatively rare thing in human life."

To see truth, like the other unique characteristics of man which we have discussed, depends on man's ability to be conscious of himself. He thus can transcend the immediate situation, and in imagination he can try to "see life steadily and see it whole." By his self-consciousness he can also search within himself, and there find the wisdom which speaks in greater or lesser degree to every man who has ears to hear.

The ancient Greeks, as Plato reports, believed that we discover truth through "reminiscence," that is by "remembering," by intuitively searching into our own experience. In the famous demonstration of this, Socrates gets an uneducated slave-boy, Meno, to prove the whole Pythagorean theorem simply by asking him questions. We do not need to accept Plato's mythological explanation—that each of us carries "ideas" implanted in the mind in a previous existence in heaven, and knowledge is a recollecting of these ideas—to agree that the phenomenon itself is a very common experience. Each of us has been observing, experiencing, "learning" a great deal more throughout our lives—probably especially in the early years—than we are aware, and we have had to lock it away in the closet of so-called unconsciousness because of the necessity of getting along with parents, teachers and social conventions. "Children and crazy people tell the truth" goes the adage—and unfortunately children soon learn not to. This "forgotten" store of wisdom is available to us as we become sufficiently clarified, sensitive, courageous and vigilant to tap it.

The popular idea that people cannot see truth because their selves get in the way is therefore false. It is not the self which makes us "see through a glass darkly" and distort what we see: it is rather the neurotic needs, repressions and conflicts. These lead us to "transfer" some prejudice or expectation of our own to other people and the world around us. Thus, it is precisely the lack of self-awareness which leads us to call error truth. The more a person lacks self-awareness, the more he is prey to anxiety and irrational anger and resentment: and while anger generally blocks us from using our more subtle intuitive means of sensing truth, anxiety always blocks us.

Also, if a person tries to rule out the self in seeing truth, if, that is, he pretends that he comes to his conclusions like a disembodied judge surveying everything from Mount Olympus, he is victim of greater delusion. Since he assumes his truth is absolute and uninfluenced by his personal interests rather than simply his most honest approximation to truth, he may become a dangerous dogmatist. Only technical issues can be true in abstraction from the immediate needs, desires and struggles of the human beings involved. In fact, one of the most common ways of avoiding seeing truth—the particular form of "resistance" generally used by intellectuals in psychotherapy—is to make an abstract or logical principle out of the problem, and generally by enough clever intellectualizing one can arrive at a fine-looking solution which is so fascinating. But, lo and behold, we later discover that all the brilliant intellectualizing did not solve the problem in reality at all, and in fact was precisely a way of avoiding the problem.

Seeing truth is a function not of the separate intellect, but of the whole man: one *experiences* truth in moving ahead as a thinking-feeling-acting unity. "We love not intellect the less" but the person more in this approach to truth. "I have been a learner all my life," writes Berdyaev in his autobiography, "but I make truth, which is universal, my own from within, through the exercise of my freedom, and my knowledge of truth is my own relation to truth."

In a previous chapter we noted Orestes' statement that as he became free from incestuous, infantile ties, he also became freer from the prejudices of Mycenae, freer from the tendency of each man to see only his own image in others' eyes and in the world around him. To be able to see truth thus goes along with emotional and ethical maturity. When one is able to see truth in this way, he gains confidence in what he says. He has become convinced of his beliefs "on his own pulse" and in his own experience, rather than through abstract principles or through being told. And he also gains humility, for he knows that since previous things he saw were partially distorted, what he now sees will also have its element of imperfection. This kind of humility does not weaken the strength of one's stand for one's own beliefs, but keeps the door open for new learning and the discovery of new truth on the morrow.

8

Man, the Transcender of Time

※

SOME READERS, however, may be raising another question. "It is all very well to discuss the goals of maturity," they may be saying, "but the clock is running out. With the world in a semipsychotic state, and the Third World War and catastrophe hovering around the corner, how can one talk about the long and steady development necessary for self-realization?"

Let us put this question concretely. Here is a young husband, for example, who was decorated as a lieutenant in the last war, and is now the editor of a newspaper. Thus he presumably has no less courage and energy than the next man. Just before going overseas he had married an attractive and talented woman. But he now painfully discovers that he and his wife have serious problems in their relationship—problems that it will take months, perhaps a couple of years, of emotional growth with the aid of psychotherapy to overcome. "Is it worth the effort and struggle," he asks himself as well as the therapist, "since I probably will be drafted again before long anyway, and after that, who knows? Maybe I should let the marriage crack up, and make out with whatever temporary relationships I happen upon for these next uncertain years."

Or here, for another example, is a brilliant young instructor in a university. He has his heart set on plans to write a book which will take perhaps five years and promises to be a considerable scientific contribution to his field. He began therapy to get help in overcoming some blockages which kept him from producing his best work. "But how can one write a book with any integrity," he wonders, "if there is no assurance of the few years time any good book takes? Possibly an atom bomb will fall on New York in the meantime—so is it worth while starting at all?" The question of time—just how late is it?—is thus the focus for the most pressing anxiety of many modern persons.

To be sure, every individual's private problems and anxiety play into this concern about the clock running out in our world. As everyone knows it is easy enough to use the insecurity of the age as an excuse for one's own neurosis. We can sigh, "The times are out of joint," and then excuse ourselves from inquiring whether something may not well be severely out of joint within ourselves.

But quite apart from the fact that our neurotic tendencies love to masquerade behind the imposing phrase, "catastrophic world situation," there remains a wide margin in which the issue raised by the questioners is entirely realistic and sound. Our world will continue in its age of anxiety for some time to come: and everyone who does not choose to play ostrich must confront that fact and learn to live with insecurity. In sophisticated circles, say of artists and intellectuals, the same apprehension expressed by the two persons above is shown in conversations on the motif, "We were born in the wrong age." In the course of such discussions, sooner or later, someone avers that it would be better to have lived in the Renaissance or in classical Athens or in Paris in the height of the Middle Ages or in some other period.

It does no good to avoid such questions by some stoical answer like, "We were born in this age and we'd better make the most of it." Let us, rather, inquire into man's relation to time—actually a very curious relation—to see whether we may gain insights which help us to make time our ally rather than our enemy.

Man Does Not Live by the Clock Alone

We have seen that one of the unique characteristics of man is that he can stand outside his present time and imagine himself ahead in the future or back in the past. A general, in planning a battle next week or next month, anticipates in fantasy how the enemy will react if attacked here or what will happen when the artillery opens up there; and thus he can prepare his army as nearly as possible for every danger by going through the battle in imagination days or weeks before it occurs.

Or a speaker in preparing an important address can—and if he is sensible he does—call to mind other times when he has given a similar speech. He reviews how the audience reacted, what parts of the address were successful and which were not, what attitude on his part was most effective and so on. By re-enacting the event in imagination, he learns from the past how better to meet the present.

This power to "look before and after" is part of man's ability to be conscious of himself. Plants and animals live by quantitative time: an hour, a week or a year past, and the tree has another ring on its trunk. But time is a quite different thing for human beings; man is the time-surmounting mammal. In his works on semantics, Alfred Korzybski has insistently made the point that the characteristic which distinguishes man from all other living things is his *time-binding* capacity. By that, says Korzybski, "I mean the capacity to use the fruits of past labors and experiences as intellectual or spiritual capital for developments in the present. . . . I mean the capacity of human beings to conduct their lives in the ever increasing light of inherited wisdom; I mean the capacity in virtue of which man is at once the heritor of the by-gone ages and the trustee of posterity."*

Psychologically and spiritually, man does not live by the clock alone. His time, rather, depends on the *significance* of the event. Yesterday, let us say, a young man spent an hour traveling on the subway each way to his work, eight hours on his relatively uninteresting job, ten minutes after work talking to a girl he has recently fallen in love with and dreams of marrying, and two hours in the evening at an adult education class. Today he remembers nothing of the two hours on the subway—it was an entirely empty experience, and he, as is

* Alfred Korzybski, *The Manhood of Humanity*. Lakeville, Conn., 1950, p. 59.

the practice of many people, had closed his eyes and tried to sleep, that is to *suspend time* until the trip was over. The eight hours on the job made only a little impression on him; of the evening class he can recall a little more. But the ten minutes with the girl occupies him most of all. He had four dreams that night—one about his class, and three about the girl. That is to say, the ten minutes with the girl takes up more "room-space" than twenty hours in the rest of the day. Psychological time is not the sheer passage of time as such, but the *meaning* of the experience, that is, what is significant for the person's hopes, anxiety, growth.

Or take a thirty-year-old adult's memories of his childhood. During the year when he was five, thousands of events happened to him. But now at thirty he can recall only three or four—the day when he went to play with his friend and the friend ran off with an older child, or the instant that morning when he saw the new tricycle under the Christmas tree, or the night his father came home drunk and struck his mother, or the afternoon his dog got lost. This is all he can recall but, interestingly enough, he remembers this handful of events which occurred twenty-five years ago more vividly than ninety-nine per cent of the events that occurred just yesterday.

Memory is not just the imprint of the past time upon us; it is the keeper of what is meaningful for our deepest hopes and fears. As such, memory is another evidence that we have a flexible and creative relation to time, the guiding principle being not the clock but the qualitative significance of our experiences.

This does not mean that quantitative time can be ignored: we have simply pointed out that we do not live by such time *alone.* Man is always part-and-parcel of the natural world, involved in nature at every point; we will rarely live over seventy or eighty years no matter what we think about it. We get old, or we get tired if we work too long at a stretch, and we cannot escape the necessity of being realistic about the clock and calendar. Man dies like every other form of life. But he is the animal who knows it and can foresee his death. By being aware of time, he can control and use it in certain ways.

The more a person is able to direct his life consciously, the more he can use time for constructive benefits. The more, however, that he is conformist, unfree, undifferentiated, the more, that is, he works not by choice but by compulsion, the more he is then the object of quantitative time. He is the servant of the time clock or whistle; he teaches such and such number of classes per week or punches so many rivets per hour, he feels bad or good depending on whether it is Monday and the beginning of a work week or Friday and the end; he gauges his rewards or lack of them on the scale of how much time he puts in. The more conformist and unfree he is, the more time is the master. He "serves time," as the amazingly accurate expression has it for being in jail. The less alive a person is—"alive" here defined as having conscious direction of his life—the more is time for him the time of the clock. The more alive he is, the more he lives by qualitative time.

"A man who lives intensely really lives," as E. E. Cummings says, "but a man who lives to be 120 doesn't necessarily live at all. You say 'I lived a whole lifetime in a moment'—a cliché that's true, and, vice versa, one takes a long train ride and it's a stinking bore. You read detective stories to kill time. If time were any good why kill it?"

Some of the anxiety on the "time is running out" theme in our day comes from something deeper than the threat of imminent war or of the H-bomb. For the passage of time in any age has the power to frighten the human being. A dog does not worry that another month or year has passed; but many people are caught up short when they think of it. They may feel that time is their archenemy, like that horrible picture of death as the grim reaper; or they sigh with relief when they say, "Time is on our side." The most obvious example of how people are frightened by time is their fear of growing older. But such fear is generally a symbol for the fact that their consciousness of time always confronts them with the question of whether they are alive, growing, or merely trying to ward off ultimate decay and extinction. I think it was C. G. Jung who said, accurately enough, that a person is afraid of growing old to the extent that he is not really living now. Hence it follows that the best way to meet the anxiety about growing old is to make sure one at the moment is fully alive.

But, even more significantly, people are afraid of time because, like being alone, it raises the specter of emptiness, of the frightening "void." On the everyday level this is shown in the fear of boredom. Man, as Erich Fromm has said, "is the only animal who can be bored"—and in that short sentence lies great import. Boredom is the "occupational disease" of being human. If a man's awareness of the passage of time tells him only that the day comes and goes and winter follows autumn and that nothing is happening in his life except hour succeeding hour, he must desensitize himself or else suffer painful boredom and emptiness. It is interesting that when we are bored, we tend to *go to sleep*—that is, to blot out consciousness, and become as nearly "extinct" as possible. Every human being experiences some boredom; a great deal of one's work, for example, must be gone through more or less by routine; but it becomes unendurable only when it has not been freely chosen or affirmed by one's self as necessary for the attainment of some greater goal.

On a not so everyday level, the anticipation of empty time can be a horror for people because they feel that if they had nothing to do, no dates and no regular plans, they would "go crazy" with uncertainty. When, because of special problems of guilt and anxiety as in the case of Macbeth, or because of inner emptiness as in the case of many people in our day, life does "signify nothing," it is indeed a reality that

> Tomorrow, and tomorrow, and tomorrow,
> Creeps in this petty pace from day to day,
> To the last syllable of recorded time;
> And all our yesterdays have lighted fools
> The way to dusty death.

In this state one's chief wish is to "blot out" time, as Shakespeare adds, or to make one's self anesthetic to it. These efforts may take the form of intoxication or—more extremely—drug addiction, or the relatively common form of trying to fill up the time to make it "pass quickly." In some languages, such as French and Greek, the expression used for going on a vacation is "I *passed* such and such time. . . ." In this country we use a similarly quantitative term, "I *spent* such and such time. . . ." It is a curious commentary on people's fear of time that if much time passes without their being aware of it, they assume they had a "good time." A "good time" is thus defined as escaping boredom. It is as though the goal were to be as little alive as possible—as though life, as Fred Allen so pungently put it, "is an unprofitable episode that disturbs an otherwise blessed state of non-existence."

One of the neurotic, unconstructive ways of using one's capacity to be aware of time is to postpone living. Man, unlike the tree and animal, is "blessed" with being able to stand outside the present and use the past or the future for escapes. The most frequently cited example of avoiding the present by living in the future is, of course, the deteriorated form of the belief that present wrongs will be righted in heaven, and that rewards and punishments will then be meted out. The tendencies in conservative religion, as in Czarist Russia, to turn people's minds from their present social and economic injustices by promises of future rewards were rightly attacked by Marx. Religion is then in actual fact an opiate, a drug for desensitizing the people.

On a more everyday level, many persons tend, when facing some problem in their present life, to remind themselves that "things will be better when I am married," or "when I graduate from college," or "when I get a new job." Indeed many people react automatically to feelings of unhappiness or ennui or purposelessness by turning their minds away from the present to the future with the question, "What pleasant thing do I have to look forward to?" Then "hope" for the future actually deadens the present. But hope need not be used in this "opiate" form. Hope in its creative and healthy sense—whether it is hope for religious fulfillment or for a happy marriage or for achievement in one's profession—can and should be an energizing attitude, the bringing of part of the joy about some future event into the present so that by anticipation, we are more alive and more able to act in the present.

Thinking of the past can, of course, have the same escape function as thinking of the future. Whenever a difficult problem appears in the present, one can say, "At least things were better at such and such a time," and let his mind bask in that memory. Indeed, so strong and universal are the tendencies to find comfort in the distant past or future that there are recurrent myths in almost every culture picturing each pole—the Garden of Eden and its variants of the longing for the happier day in a state of childlike innocence, and the myths of paradise ahead in the form of heaven or the earthly utopia of those who believe in perpetual, automatic progress.

As living in hopes for the future is said to be the usual escape of unsophisticated people, so living in the past may be the common escape of sophisticated persons. In therapy this type knows that it is not *de mode* to flee into hopes of future rewards in heaven, but they have learned that it is entirely respectable to talk about the past: for do not one's basic problems have their roots in early childhood? This truth can then be used as a neat rationalization. For when a person comes to a session after a quarrel with his wife, he can then leap back into talking about what his mother did to him in his early childhood, or how he got on with his first girl friend. This is often easier for him than to confront the immediate question of what caused the quarrel and what are his motives in his present relation with his wife. Fortunately the therapist can generally tell whether the person is using his past as an escape (in which case to talk about it will never make any psychological change in him) or as a source of illumination and a release of dynamic for the present.

Let us turn now to the constructive ways of surmounting time. No doubt some readers have already been saying, "But one can be unaware of the passage of time because one is so alive in the present moment, not just because one puts one's self into a stupor to escape time." True. In the latter case, an hour is like a week because it lumbers so slowly and painfully: in the former—being unaware of time because of the heightened aliveness of the moment—an hour is like a week because it gives as much joy and happiness.

An excellent picture of the struggle to transcend time is painted by Goethe in his drama *Faust*. Faust has made his compact with the devil, Mephistopheles, because he is bored, dissatisfied, "fed up," ungratified by this activity or that, unable to find a way of life which gives him any sense of lasting worth. Indeed, the folk saying that the devil has work for idle hands is put in much more poetic form by Goethe when he has Mephistopheles say, in so many words, that for him Time is "complete monotony."

What good for us, this endlessly creating. . . .
'Tis just the same as if it ne'er existed,
Yet goes in circles round as if it had, however:
I'd rather choose, instead, the Void forever.

How more vividly could it be stated that the kingdom of Mephistopheles is the kingdom of *monotony* and the *void*!

As the story progresses, Faust is given everything he desires—his
sweetheart Margaret, later Helen of Troy, then knowledge, power,
and eventually he becomes chancellor to the emperor. Then as an old
man he undertakes to construct dikes to push the sea back so that in
place of stagnant swamps, green fields appear. The men in his land
can then till the soil and raise their food, and their herds grow fat on
the rich land. When Faust notes the joy of the people because of his
deed of cultural and natural creativity, he suddenly experiences what
he never had before, the joy of the eternal moment,

Then dared I hail the Moment fleeing:
'Ah, still delay—thou art so fair!'
The traces cannot, of mine earthly being,
In aeons perish—they are there!—
In proud fore-feeling of such lofty bliss,
I now enjoy the highest Moment—this!

These words of Faust, that in his act the "traces of his earthly
being" have an eternal significance, lead us to inquire, how does one
find the meaning of the "fleeing moment"?

The Pregnant Moment

The first thing necessary for a constructive dealing with time is to
learn to live in the reality of the present moment. For psychologically
speaking, this present moment is all we have. The past and future
have meaning because they are part of the present: a past event has

existence now because you are thinking of it at this present moment, or because it influences you so that you, as a living being in the present, are that much different. The future has reality because one can bring it into his mind in the present. Past was the present at one time, and the future will be the present at some coming moment. To try to live in the "when" of the future or the "then" of the past always involves an artificiality, a separating one's self from reality; for in actuality one exists in the present. The past has meaning as it lights up the present, and the future as it makes the present richer and more profound.

When a person looks directly into himself, all he is aware of is his instant of consciousness at that particular moment of the present. It is this instant of consciousness which is most real, and must not be fled from.

Dr. Otto Rank was the therapist who most persuasively pointed out that the past and future live in the psychological present. In the 1920's, orthodox psychoanalysis was bogging down in artificial excursions into the past which lacked reality and dynamic and were in danger of becoming the same deadening intellectual exercises, interesting as archeological explorations but without power to change anyone's life, for which Freud had attacked academicians. Rank jarred psychotherapy back to reality by showing that whatever is significant in a person's past—such as in early childhood relations—will be brought into his present relationships. His early relations with father and mother appear in the present in his way of treating therapist, wife and employer (what Freud aptly called "transference"). One does not need merely to *talk* about such past relations in therapy. In actions which speak louder than words, the basic conflicts emerge directly in the consulting room in the anger, dependency, love or what not that the patient feels toward the therapist—though he, the patient, may not be aware at the time that this is what he is acting out. This is why in therapy "experiencing" is always more powerful and curative than talking *about* experiences.

It is by no means as easy as it may look to live in the immediate present. For it requires a high degree of awareness of one's self as an experiencing "I." The less one is conscious of himself as the one who acts, that is, the more unfree and automatic he is, the less he will be aware of the immediate present. As one person who was trying to avoid boredom in a meaningless routine job described it, "I work as though I were someone else, not myself." In such situations we feel as though we were "a million miles away" from what we are doing, acting as though in a "daze" or as though in a dream or "half asleep" or as though there were a wall between one's self and the present.

But the more awareness one has—that is, the more he experiences himself as the acting, directing agent in what he is doing—the more alive he will be and the more responsive to the present moment. Like self-awareness itself, this experiencing of the reality of the present can be cultivated. It is often useful to ask one's self, "What do I experience at this very moment?" Or "Where am I—what is most significant to me emotionally—at this given moment?"

To confront the reality of the present moment often produces anxiety. On the most basic level, this anxiety is a kind of vague experience of being "naked"; it is the feeling of being face to face with some important reality before which one cannot flinch and from which one cannot retreat or hide. It is like the feeling one might have in coming suddenly face to face with a person one loved and admired: one is confronted with an intense relationship one must react to, do something about. It is an intensity of experience, this immediate and direct confronting of the reality of the moment, similar to intense creative activity, and it carries with it the same nakedness and creative anxiety as well as the same joy.

The more obvious reason why confronting the present produces anxiety is that it raises the question of decisions and responsibility. One can't do much about the past, and very little about the distant future—how pleasant, then, to dream about them! How free from bother, how relieved from troublesome thoughts about what one has to do with one's life! The man who has quarreled with his wife can talk of his mother with relief, but to consider the quarrel with his wife sooner or later entails the question of what he proposes to do about it? It is easier to dream of "when I get married" than to face the question, "Why don't I do something about my social life now?";

simpler to muse of "my future job when I get out of college" than to ask why one's studies are not more vital at the moment, and what are one's motives for being in college anyway.

The most effective way to ensure the value of the future, as we have mentioned, is to confront the present courageously and constructively. For the future is born out of and made by the present. Faust states the truth in the quotation above that "the traces of his earthly being would outlast aeons." That is to say, every creative act has its eternal aspect. This is not by ecclesiastical fiat, or merely because of the "immortality of influence," but because, as we have shown in the section above, an essential characteristic of the creative act done in human consciousness is that it is not limited by quantitative time. No one values a painting according to how long it took to paint it or how big it is: should we judge our actions by more superficial standards than a painting?

This brings us to the deteriorated forms of the religious idea of "eternal life." The phrase "eternal life" is popularly used to imply endless time, as though eternity meant going on year after year limitlessly. One sees this view implied in the question frequently painted by some persons—with what motives heaven only knows—on the sides of buildings to challenge the passer-by on the highways, "Where will you spend eternity?" This is an odd question when you think about it. "Spend" implies a given quantity—if you spend half your money, you have only half left; and could one "spend" half or two-thirds of eternity? Such a view of eternity is not only repugnant psychologically—what a boring prospect, that one spend year after year endlessly!—but it is also absurd logically and unsound theologically. Eternity is not a given quantity of time: it transcends time. Eternity is the qualitative significance of time. One doesn't have to identify the experience of listening to music with the theological meaning of eternity to realize that in music—or in love, or in any work which proceeds from one's inner integrity—that the "eternal" is a way of relating to life, not a succession of "tomorrows."

Hence Jesus proclaimed, "the Kingdom of Heaven is within you." That is to say, your experience of eternity will be found in how you relate to each given moment—or not at all. Goethe echoes the same truth in putting into Faust's mouth the phrase, *"Fore-feeling* of such lofty bliss": eternity comes into the present moment as a quality of existence.

The deteriorated uses of the term "eternal" have caused many intelligent people to avoid it. And that has been unfortunate, for it has meant omitting an important side of human experience, and constricting our views psychologically and philosophically. "The problem of time may well be the fundamental problem of philosophy," writes Berdyaev. "An instant in time," he adds, "possesses value to the extent to which it is united to eternity and provides an issue out of the issuelessness of time—only in virtue of being an atom of eternity . . ."*

The present moment is thus not limited from one point on the clock to another. It is always "pregnant," always ready to open, to give birth. One has only to try the experiment of looking deeply within himself, let us say, trailing almost any random idea, and he will find, so rich is a moment of consciousness in the human mind, that associations and new ideas beckon in every direction. Or take a dream—it occurred in just one flash of consciousness as the alarm went off, yet it might take many minutes for you to tell all it pictured. To be sure, one picks and chooses. One does not live out his dreams or fantasies—except temporarily, if he is composing music, or in a psychoanalytic session, or constructing some plan in fantasy for his work. And even then he keeps a clear awareness of the relation of the beckoning possibilities which are being uncovered to actual reality. Thus the moment always has its "finite" side, to use a philosophical term, which the mature person never forgets. But the moment also always has its infinite side, it always beckons with new possibilities. Time for the human being is not a corridor; it is a continual opening out.

"In the Light of Eternity"

There are many experiences which jar us out of the quantitative, routine treadmill of time, but chief among them is the thought of dying.

* Nicolai Berdyaev, *Spirit and Reality.* New York, Charles Scribner's Sons, 1935.

A modern English author describes how he endeavored for years to write by following conventional methods. "I thought I could write to formula," as he put it; and during those years he plodded along at a mediocre level. But during the war, he continued, "I found out why I had not been published before. . . . When we were all thinking we might die the next day, I decided to write what I wanted."

When we point out, as actually happened, that his writing then became successful, some persons might interpret the illustration with a conventional success moral, "If you wish to be successful, write what you want." But such a moral, of course, entirely misses the point. The author's previous need to write according to external standards and for ulterior purposes—success being the chief one in our day—was exactly what was blocking him in tapping his qualities and powers as a writer. And it was precisely this need that he gave up at the time of facing death. If one may die tomorrow, why knock one's self out trying to fit this standard or that formula? Assuming that success and rewards might be achieved by writing to formula—which is a toss-up in any case—one may not be around long enough anyway to enjoy the rewards, so why not treat one's self to the joy at the moment of writing according to one's own integrity?

The possibility of death jars us loose from the treadmill of time because it so vividly reminds us that we do not go on endlessly. It shocks us into taking the present seriously; the Turkish proverb employed to rationalize procrastination, "Tomorrow also is a blessed day," no longer comforts and excuses; one cannot wait around forever. It makes more crucial for us the fact that while we are not dead at the moment, we some time will be: so why not choose something at least interesting in the meantime? The so-called cynical poet of the Old Testament, Ecclesiastes, is in fact very realistic at this point. Amid his recurrent refrain, "all is vanity," he points out that the wise man will not wait around for future rewards and punishments. "Whatsoever thy hand findeth to do," Ecclesiastes continues, "do it with thy might; for there is no work, nor substance, nor knowledge, nor wisdom in the grave whither thou goest."

Spinoza was fond of saying that a man should act *sub specie aeternitatis*—under the form of eternity. "For I understand Eternity," he writes, "to be existence itself. . . . For the existence of a thing, such as an eternal truth . . . cannot be explained by duration or time. . . ." He goes on to say that the existence of something depends on its essence—an idea which isn't as abstruse as it sounds at first glance. To apply it to one's self, a person acts "under the form of eternity" to the extent that his actions arise from his own essential center. In the example of the author above, such an act was his decision to write, not according to external changing fads, which rise and fall from week to week, but from the inward, unique, original character which makes him an individual. Living in the eternal moment does not mean mere *intensity* of living (though self-awareness always adds some intensity to one's experience): nor does it mean living by an absolute dogma, religious or otherwise, or by a moral rule. It means, rather, making one's decisions in freedom and responsibility, in self-awareness and in accord with one's own unique character as a person.

No Matter What the Age

Our discussion in this chapter leads us to the conclusion that, on the deepest level, the question of which age we live in is irrelevant.

The basic question is how the individual, in his own awareness of himself and the period he lives in, is able through his decisions to attain inner freedom and to live according to his own inner integrity. Whether we live in the Renaissance, or in thirteenth-century France, or at the time of the fall of Rome, we are part-and-parcel of our age in every respect—its wars, its economic conflicts, its anxiety, its achievement. But no "well-integrated" society can perform for the individual, or relieve him from, his task of achieving self-consciousness and the capacity for making his own choices responsibly. And no traumatic world situation can rob the individual of the privilege of making the final decision with regard to himself, even if it is only to affirm his own fate. It may have been superficially easier for a person to be "adjusted" in another age—those "golden ages" of Greece or the

Renaissance that one might look back to longingly. But the wish that one lived in those times, except as an exercise in fantasy, is based on a false understanding of man's relation to time. In those days it might actually *not* have been any easier for the individual to find and choose to be himself. In our day there is greater need for one to come to terms with one's self; we are less able to "rest in the mothering arms" of our historical period. So could one not argue, if it were a matter for drawing-room argument, that it is better for a person's learning to find himself to live in our day? On the superficial level there are assets or debits to living in any period. On the more profound level, each individual must come to his own consciousness of himself, and he does this on a level which transcends the particular age he lives in.

The same holds true for one's chronological age. The important issue is not whether a person is twenty or forty or sixty: it rather is whether he fulfills his own capacity of self-conscious choice at his particular level of development. This is why a healthy child at eight— as everyone has observed—can be more of a person than a neurotic adult of thirty. The child is not more mature in a chronological sense, nor can he do as much as the adult, nor take care of himself as well, but he is more mature when we judge maturity by honesty of emotion, originality, and capacity to make choices on matters adequate to his stage of development. The statement of the person of twenty who says, "I will begin to live when I am thirty-five" is as falsely based as the one who, at forty or fifty, laments, "I cannot live because I have lost my youth." Interestingly enough, one generally finds on closer inspection that this is the same person, that the *one who makes that lament at fifty was postponing living also at twenty*—which demonstrates our point even more incisively.

This transcending of time is illustrated again in the drama of Orestes. In his tragic struggle to become free from the incestuous circle, as we observed it in Chapter 4, Orestes was able to some extent to overcome the tendency to "see only himself in others' eyes," and thus to see truth to some degree objectively and to "love outwardly." These are all ways of living *sub specie aeternitatis;* they show the human being's capacity to transcend the given situation of the moment. They involve transcending Mycenae, or, as Orestes symbolically expresses it, walking out of the limits of the city, "toward humanity." When Orestes has left the stage in the last sentences of Jeffers' version of the drama, the concluding words, referring to the young man's eventual death, express our point exactly:

> . . . But young or old, few years or many, signified less than
>   nothing
> To him who had climbed the tower beyond time, consciously. . . .*

The task and possibility of the human being is to move from his original situation as an unthinking and unfree part of the mass, whether this mass is his actual early existence as a foetus or his being symbolically a part of the mass in a conformist, automaton society—to move from the womb, that is, through the incestuous circle, which is but one step removed from the womb, through the experience of the birth of self-awareness, the crises of growth, the struggles, choices and advances from the familiar to the unfamiliar, to ever-widening consciousness of himself and thus ever-widening freedom and responsibility, to higher levels of differentiation in which he progressively integrates himself with others in freely chosen love and creative work. Each step in this journey means that he lives less as a servant of automatic time and more as one who transcends time, that is, one who lives by meaning which he chooses. Thus the person who can die courageously at thirty—who has attained a degree of freedom and differentiation that he can face courageously the necessity of giving up his life—is more mature than the person who on his deathbed at eighty cringes and begs still to be shielded from reality.

The practical implication is that one's goal is to live each moment with freedom, honesty and responsibility. One is then in each moment fulfilling so far as he can his own nature and his evolutionary task.

---

* "Tower Beyond Tragedy" from *Roan Stallion*. Reprinted by permission of Random House, Inc. Copyright 1925 by Boni & Liveright.

In this way one experiences the joy and gratification that accompany fulfilling one's own nature. Whether the young instructor eventually completes his book or not is a secondary question: the primary issue is whether he, or anyone else, writes and thinks in the given sentence or paragraph what he believes will "gain the praise of another," or what he himself believes is true and honest according to his lights at the moment. The young husband, to be sure, cannot be certain of his relation with his wife five years hence: but in the best of historical periods, could one ever have been certain that he would live out the week or month? *Does not the uncertainty of our time teach us the most important lesson of all—that the ultimate criteria are the honesty, integrity, courage and love of a given moment of relatedness?* If we do not have that, we are not building for the future anyway; if we do have it, we can trust the future to itself.

The qualities of freedom, responsibility, courage, love and inner integrity are ideal qualities, never perfectly realized by anyone, but they are the psychological goals which give meaning to our movement toward integration. When Socrates was describing the ideal way of life and the ideal society, Glaucon countered: "Socrates, I do not believe that there is such a City of God anywhere on earth." Socrates answered, "Whether such a city exists in heaven or ever will exist on earth, the wise man will live after the manner of that city, having nothing to do with any other, and in so looking upon it, will set his own house in order."

Index